한국어 발음

연세대학교 한국어학당 편

Copyright ©1995 by Korean Language Institute of Yonsei University
All rigts reserved.
Not to be reproduced without author's permission.

Foreword

We often call our era the Information Age. In it people will do anything to get more information. In conversation many will try to get only the information they feel necessary. Increasingly more people are satisfied with a less than thorough understanding of what has been said, paying no attention to grammar and pronunciation. Considering the influence of pronunciation and intonation, however, these are elements that cannot be ignored in language education.

Language expression is achieved with the tools of script and sound. We all practice handwriting from an early age, being told that handwriting reflects the face and mind of the writer. Since pronunciation is also a tool of expression it goes without saying that it must be practiced properly according to established rules. This is because even within the range of the same language, the effect ones speech carries differs according to choice of standard language or regional dialect, and ones education, level of refinement, and character are judged by accuracy of pronunciation.

Pronunciation is also important in learning Korean as a foreign language. Near native pronunciation is like an extra topping of perfection complementing accurate sentences that respect grammatical rules. To this end not only should the accurate rendering of each phoneme be taught from the beginning stages of Korean education, but the various aspects of the pronunciation of consonants must be systematically learned as well, phonetic phenomena such as differentiation between voiced and voiceless sounds, vocalization, and prolonged sounds.

This year marks thirty six years of Korean language education for foreigners at Yonsei University's Korean Language Institute. During this time the Korean Language Institute has played a pioneering role in the development of Korean as a foreign language education not only in Korea but around the world by writing various Korean language textbooks for use in such education. It is a joy to be able to continue our tradition of leadership in Korean language education with this pronunciation textbook. It will be of help to foreigners learning Korean pronunciation, and a point of reference for Korean language teachers seeking to teach pronunciation more systematically.

This book was made possible by the efforts of Mrs. Hong, Kyungpyo, who has dedicated her life to Korean language education. She has prepared this textbook in an effort to help solve easily and step by step the different problems of pronunciation that confront both speakers of English and speakers of Japanese. We wish to express our appreciation to Mrs. Hong and to thank all the members of the Textbook Publication Committee who worked so hard in its preparation.

May 1995

Yonsei University
Korean Language Institute
Textbook Publication Committee

Preface

We use language to convey our thoughts to others. Language is conveyed by speech sounds; if these sounds are unclear, communication with one's interlocutor fails. This allows us to say that pronunciation is of prime importance when learning a foreign language, and that pronunciation training is the first priority in the foreign language learning process.

If one wishes to acquire precise pronunciation habits in a foreign language, one must be well acquainted with the overall phonological system of the language in question. Thus, this book aims to introduce the Korean sound system to foreigners learning Korean as a second language in as easy and straightforward a manner as possible.

This book is designed for:

   a) beginners in the Korean language,
   b) examination, correction and systematic adjustment of pronunciation for those who have already studied Korean,
   c) teachers of Korean as a foreign language.

The book is laid out in a step-by-step fashion, such that the student progresses from one unit to the next after completing the generous practice exercises included for each pronunciation point. Thus, the exercises in Lesson One treat the vowels, the exercises after the section on consonantal phonology treat consonants and vowels, the exercises following the section on syllable-final consonants (*patčhim*) treat all three of these, and finally, Lesson Four includes comprehensive review exercises.

The book also includes exercises which compare and contrast those sounds most difficult to pronounce because of interference or transfer-phenomena which occur when a native English speaker learns Korean.

In addition, the book includes many charts and tables to aid memorization and make the book easier on the eyes.

Kyung Pyo HONG, Yonsei University

Note from the Translator

I have tried to follow Mrs. Hong's Korean presentation as closely as possible, and in some cases retain and/or include the original Korean terminology for certain well-known pronunciation phenomena. Individual Korean words given to exemplify pronunciation points in the text are left untranslated, but I have given rough translations for all sentence-length Korean examples from the exericses.

Translated by: Dr. Ross King, SOAS

TABLE OF CONTENTS

Foreword • 1

Preface • 3

I. 한글 — The Korean Alphabet 11

II. The Phonemes of Korean 13

    Lesson One: The Vowels. 15
        1. Simple Vowels 15
            Exercise 1 17
        2. Diphthongs 19
            Exercise 2 21

    Lesson Two: The Consonants 22
        1. Distinctions according to Manner of Articulation 22
            Exercise 3 25
        2. Distinctions according to Place
            of Articulation 27

    Lesson Three: Combinations of Vowel and Consonant 28
            Exercise 4.1 29
            Exercise 4.2 31

Exercise 4.3 33
Exercise 4.4 35
Exercise 4.5 37

LESSON FOUR: Syllable-Final Sounds (*patčhim*) 39
  1. *patčhim*: 39
    Exercise 5 46
    Exercise 6 48
  2. Complex *patčhim* 51
    Exercise 7 54
    Exercise 8 56
    Exercise 9 59
    Exercise 10 61
    Exercise 11 63
    Exercise 12 64
    Exercise 13 67

LESSON FIVE: Voiced and Voiceless Consonants 68
    Exercise 14 70

III. Phonological Changes 73

LESSON SIX: Vowel Harmony 75
  1. Bright Vowels (*Yangsŏng* Vowels) 76
  2. Dark Vowels (*Ŭmsŏng* Vowels) 76
    Exercise 15 78

LESSON SEVEN: Contraction and Loss 79
  1. Contraction 79
  2. Loss 81
    Exercise 16 84

LESSON EIGHT: Consonant Assimilations 86
  1. /p, t, k + m, n / → [m, n, ŋ + m, n] 87
  2. /m, ŋ + l / → [m, ŋ + n] 88

3. /p, k + l / →[p, k + n] → [m, ŋ + n].............................. 89
　　4. /n + l / → [n + n]... 89
　　5. /n + l, l + n / → [l + l , l + l].. 89
　　　　Exercise 17.. 91
　　　　Exercise 18.. 94

LESSON NINE: Tensification and Voicing.............................. 96
　　1. When Voiceless Sounds meet 96
　　2. When Voiceless Consonants meet Voiced
　　　　Consonants... 98
　　　　Exercise 19.. 102

LESSON TEN: Aspiration 106
　　1. /p + h/ → [pʰ]... 106
　　2. /t + h, h + t/ → [tʰ]... 107
　　3. /ts + h, h + ts/ → [tsʰ].. 107
　　4. /k + h, h + k/ → [kʰ]... 107
　　　　Exercise 20.. 109
　　　　Exercise 21.. 110

LESSON ELEVEN: Palatalization... 112
　　1. /t + i/ → [tsi] 112
　　2. /tʰ + i/ → [tsʰi]... 112
　　3. /t + h + i/ → [tsʰi].. 113
　　　　Exercise 22.. 114
　　　　Exercise 23.. 116

IV. Intrusive ㅅ and ㄴ 119

LESSON TWELVE: Insertion of ㅅ and ㄴ 121
　　1. ㅅ Insertion 121
　　2. ㄴ Insertion 122
　　　　Exercise 24.. 126

8 / Table of Contents

V. Prosodic Features 129

    LESSON THIRTEEN: Length, Pitch and Stress 131
        1. Length 131
        2. Pitch 132
        3. Stress 133
            Exercise 25 135

Index 137

Charts and Tables

Chart 1: *Han'gŭl*. 12

Chart 2: Simple Vowels 16

Chart 3: Consonants 22

Chart 4: Consonant Contrasts 23

Chart 5: Syllable-Final Consonants (*patchim*) 51

Chart 6: Vowel Harmony 75

Chart 7: Contractions 79

Chart 8: Loss 81

Chart 9: Consonant Assimilation 86

Chart 10: Tensification 96

Chart 11: Voicing and Tensification 98

Chart 12: Aspiration 106

I.
한글 – The Korean Alphabet

Han'gŭl (originally called *Hunmin Chŏngŭm*) was promulgated in the 28th year of the reign of King Sejong, 4th monarch of the *Chosŏn* dynasty. The *Hunmin Chŏngŭm* consisted of 11 vowel signs and 17 consonant signs, giving a total of 28 signs. The letter shapes for the vowels were based on the East Asian philosophy of divination (the I *Ching or Book of Changes*), and used the three elements Heaven, Earth and Man. The letter shapes for the consonants were based on graphic imitations of the human articulatory organs.

The Draft *Han'gŭl* Unified Orthography (*Han'gŭl Match'umpŏp T'ongil-an*) announced by the *Chosŏnŏ Hakhoe* (Korean Language Society, former name of the *Han'gŭl Hakhoe*) on October 29, 1933, consists of 10 vowel signs and 14 consonant signs, and has remained in use to this day. The letters' names and alphabetical order are as follows:

Vowels :   ㅏ (아)   ㅑ (야)   ㅓ (어)   ㅕ (여)   ㅗ (오)   ㅛ (요)
          ㅜ (우)   ㅠ (유)   ㅡ (으)   ㅣ (이)

Consonants: ㄱ (기역)   ㄴ (니은)   ㄷ (디귿)   ㄹ (리을)   ㅁ (미음)
              ㅂ (비읍)   ㅅ (시옷)   ㅇ (이응)   ㅈ (지읒)   ㅊ (치읓)
              ㅋ (키읔)   ㅌ (티읕)   ㅍ (피읖)   ㅎ (히읗)

The Korean language is a distant cousin of the Altaic language family. In terms of its morphological characteristics, Korean is an agglutinating language.

Chart 1. *Han'gŭl* (The Korean Alphabet)

모음 자음	ㅏ [a]	ㅑ [ja]	ㅓ [ɔ]	ㅕ [jɔ]	ㅗ [o]	ㅛ [jo]	ㅜ [u]	ㅠ [ju]	ㅡ [ɨ]	ㅣ [i]
ㄱ [k/g]	가	갸	거	겨	고	교	구	규	그	기
ㄴ [n]	나	냐	너	녀	노	뇨	누	뉴	느	니
ㄷ [t/d]	다	댜	더	뎌	도	됴	두	듀	드	디
ㄹ [r/l]	라	랴	러	려	로	료	루	류	르	리
ㅁ [m]	마	먀	머	며	모	묘	무	뮤	므	미
ㅂ [p/b]	바	뱌	버	벼	보	뵤	부	뷰	브	비
ㅅ [s]	사	샤	서	셔	소	쇼	수	슈	스	시
ㅇ [ŋ]	아	야	어	여	오	요	우	유	으	이
ㅈ [ts/dz]	자	쟈	저	져	조	죠	주	쥬	즈	지
ㅊ [tsʰ]	차	챠	처	쳐	초	쵸	추	츄	츠	치
ㅋ [kʰ]	카	캬	커	켜	코	쿄	쿠	큐	크	키
ㅌ [tʰ]	타	탸	터	텨	토	툐	투	튜	트	티
ㅍ [pʰ]	파	퍄	퍼	펴	포	표	푸	퓨	프	피
ㅎ [h]	하	햐	허	혀	호	효	후	휴	흐	히

II.
The Phonemes of Korean

The Korean phonemes divide into Vowels and Consonants. Vowels can be pronounced alone, but consonants cannot—they always combine with a vowel in order to produce a sound (this is why they are called con-sonants).

Korean syllable types are as follows:

1. | V | ...이 [i]

2. | C | V | ...ㅍ [pʰ] + ㅏ [a] → 파 [pʰa]

3. | V | C | ...이 [i] + ㅂ [p] → 입 [ip]

4. | C | V | C | ...ㅍ [pʰ] + ㅏ [a] + ㄹ [l] → 팔 [pʰal]

　*v = vowel
　 c = consonant

Lesson One

The Vowels

Vowels are sounds produced by manipulating the vibrations within the vocal tract which are produced by air from the lungs passing unobstructed across the vocal chords. Korean has 10 simple vowels and 11 diphthongs.

1. Simple Vowels

The simple vowels are 아[a], 어[ɔ], 오[o], 우[u], 으[ɨ], 이[i], 애[ɛ], 에[e], 외[ö], 위[ü], but the vowels 외 and 위 can also be pronounced as diphthongs([we] and [wi], respectively). Simple vowels are pronounced the same from beginning to finish. They are distinguished from each other by adjustments in tongue position (front or back), degree of mouth aperture and lip rounding.

Vowels pronounced
    at the front of the tongue   are called   front vowels
    at the middle of the tongue   are called   mid vowels
    at the back of the tongue   are called   back vowels

Vowels pronounced with
    mouth slightly open and tongue   high   are   high vowels
    mouth more open and tongue   middle   are   central vowels
    mouth wide open and tongue   low   are   low vowels

Vowels pronounced
    with rounded lips   are called   rounded vowels
    with unrounded lips   are called   unrounded vowels

II. The Phonemes of Korean

The distinctions above can be expressed in a chart as follows:

Chart 2. **Simple Vowels**

Tongue Position / Tongue Height	FRONT	MID	BACK
High V	ㅣ [i] (ㅟ) [ü]	ㅡ [ɨ]	(ㅜ) [u]
Central V	ㅔ [e] (ㅚ) [ö]	ㅓ [ɔ]	(ㅗ) [o]
Low V	ㅐ [ɛ]	ㅏ [a]	

*Vowels in parentheses ( ) are rounded vowels.

In order to produce the simple vowels simply and exactly, you should practice them in the following order:

High Vowels :   이 [i] → 위 [ü] → 으 [ɨ] → 우 [u]
Central Vowels: (이 [i]) → 에 [e] → 외 [ö] → 어 [ɔ] → 오 [o]
Low Vowels: (이 [i]) →(에 [e])→ 애 [ɛ] → 아 [a]
Front vowels: 이 [i] → 에 [e] → 애 [ɛ]
                이 [i] → 위 [ü] → 외 [ö]
Mid Vowels :   (이 [i]) → 으 [ɨ] → 어 [ɔ] → 아 [a]
Back Vowels: (이 [i]) →(으 [ɨ])→ 우 [u] → 오 [o]

Exercise 1. Practice pronouncing the simple vowels.

1. 이 위 으 우

   이이이 위위위 으으으 우우우, 우우우 으으으 위위위 이이이
   이위으우, 이위으우, 이위으우, 우으위이, 우으위이, 우으위이
   이위으우으위이, 이위으우으위이, 이위으우으위이, 이위으우으위이,
   이위으우으위이

2. 에 외 어 오

   이이이 에에에 외외외 어어어 오오오, 오오오 어어어 외외외
   에에에 이이이
   이에외어오, 이에외어오, 이에외어오, 오어외에이, 오어외에이,
   오어외에이
   이에외어오어외에이, 이에외어오어외에이, 이에외어오어외에이,
   이에외어오어외에이, 이에외어오어외에이
   에외어오어외에, 에외어오어외에, 에외어오어외에, 에외어오어외에,
   에외어오어외에

3. 애 아

   이이이 에에에 애애애 아아아, 아아아 애애애 에에에 이이이
   이에애아, 이에애아, 이에애아, 아애에이, 아애에이, 아애에이
   이에애아애에이, 이에애아애에이, 이에애아애에이, 이에애아애에이,
   이에애아애에이
   애아애, 애아애, 애아애, 애아애, 애아애

4. 이 에 애

   이이이 에에에 애애애, 애애애 에에에 이이이
   이에애, 이에애, 이에애, 애에이, 애에이, 애에이
   이에애에이, 이에애에이, 이에애에이, 이에애에이, 이에애에이

18 / II. The Phonemes of Korean

5. 으 어 아

이이이 위위위 으으으 어어어 아아아,
아아아 어어어 으으으 위위위 이이이
이위으어아,   이위으어아,   이위으어아,
아어으위이,   아어으위이,   아어으위이
이위으어아어으위이,   이위으어아어으위이,   이위으어아어으위이,
이위으어아어으위이,   이위으어아어으위이
으어아어으,   으어아어으,   으어아어으,
으어아어으,   으어아어으

6. 우 오

이이이 위위위 으으으 우우우 오오오,   오오오 우우우 으으으
위위위 이이이
이위으우오,   이위으우오,   이위으우오,
오우으위이,   오우으위이,   오우으위이
이위으우오우으위이,   이위으우오우으위이,   이위으우오우으위이,
이위으우오우으위이,   이위으우오우으위이
우오우,   우오우,   우오우,   우오우,   우오우

2. Diphthongs

Diphthongs are vowels which are modified in the course of pronunciation: either by changing the shape of the lips or the position of the tongue. 외 and 위 can be pronounced either as single vowels or as diphthongs.

Diphthongs which start with
the tongue position of 이 : 야[ja], 여[jɔ], 요[jo], 유[ju],
애[jɛ], 예[je]
오 : 와[wa], 왜[wɛ]
우 : 워[wɔ], 웨[we]
으 and finish in the position of 이 : 의[ɨi]

In order to pronounce the diphthongs easily and exactly, you should practice them in the following order.

a) 아 [a] → 야 [ja]   어 [ɔ] → 여 [jɔ]
   오 [o] → 요 [jo]   우 [u] → 유 [ju]
   애 [ɛ] → 얘 [jɛ]   에 [e] → 예 [je]

b) 오 [o] + 아 [a] → 와 [wa]
   오 [o] + 애 [ɛ] → 왜 [wɛ]

c) 우 [u] + 어 [ɔ] → 워 [wɔ]
   우 [u] + 에 [e] → 웨 [we]

d) 으 [ɨ] + 이 [i] → 의 [ɨi]*

* '의' is pronounced in the following ways:

a) as the first sound of a syllable, like 의[ɨi]
   의자 의사 의무 의리 의미

b) after an initial consonant, like ㅣ [i]

　　무늬　유희　띄어쓰기　희다　희미하다

c) in any non-initial syllable, like ㅢ[ii] or ㅣ [i]

　　회의　거의　주의　의의　토의하다

d) the possessive particle written 의 is pronounced ㅢ[ii] or ㅔ [e]

　　우리의 시조　그녀의 머리　나라의 소유　민주주의의 의의

Lesson One: The Vowels / 21

Exercise 2. Practice pronouncing the diphthongs.

1. 야
   아야, 아야, 아야, 아야, 아야,   야, 야, 야, 야, 야

2. 여
   어여, 어여, 어여, 어여, 어여,   여, 여, 여, 여, 여

3. 요
   오요, 오요, 오요, 오요, 오요,   요, 요, 요, 요, 요

4. 유
   우유, 우유, 우유, 우유, 우유,   유, 유, 유, 유, 유

5. 얘
   애얘, 애얘, 애얘, 애얘, 애얘,   얘, 얘, 얘, 얘, 얘

6. 예
   에예, 에예, 에예, 에예, 에예,   예, 예, 예, 예, 예

7. 와
   오아, 오아, 오아, 오아, 오아,   와, 와, 와, 와, 와

8. 왜
   오애, 오애, 오애, 오애, 오애,   왜, 왜, 왜, 왜, 왜

9. 워
   우어, 우어, 우어, 우어, 우어,   워, 워, 워, 워, 워

10. 웨
    우에, 우에, 우에, 우에, 우에,   웨, 웨, 웨, 웨, 웨

11. 의
    으이, 으이, 으이, 으이, 으이,   의, 의, 의, 의, 의

Lesson Two

The Consonants

Korean has 19 consonants. They are distinguished according to the place and manner of articulation, as in the following chart:

Chart 3. **Consonants**

Place of articulation / Manner of articulation			Bilabial	Tongue-tip Alveolar	Alveo-Palatal	Velar	Glottal
Voiceless	Plosives	Plain	ㅂ [p/b]	ㄷ [t/d]		ㄱ [k/g]	
		Tense	ㅃ [p']	ㄸ [t']		ㄲ [k']	
		Aspirated	ㅍ [pʰ]	ㅌ [tʰ]		ㅋ [kʰ]	
	Affricates	Plain			ㅈ [ts]		
		Tense			ㅉ [ts']		
		Aspirated			ㅊ [tsʰ]		
	Fricatives	Plain		ㅅ [s]			ㅎ [h]
		Tense		ㅆ [s']			
Voiced	Nasal		ㅁ [m]	ㄴ [n]		ㅇ [ŋ]	
	Liquid			ㄹ [r,l]			

1. Distinctions according to Manner of Articulation

Consonants can be divided into voiced and voiceless types; in Korean, all the vowels and /ㅁ, ㄴ, ㅇ, ㄹ/ are inherently voiced sounds. Within the voiceless consonants, there are plosives, affricates, and fricatives. Within the voiced consonants, there are nasals and liquids. The plosives, affricates and fricatives can be further divided into Plain, Tense and Aspirated types.

Plosives are sounds which block momentarily the stream of air from the lungs.

Fricatives are sounds produced by the friction made by narrowing, but not completely blocking, the passage of air within the mouth or between the vocal chords.

Affricates are sounds which begin as a plosive and finish as a fricative.

1) Plain, Tense and Aspirated Consonants

The Plain consonants are made keeping the muscles of the vocal organs in their normal state, and are /p, t, ts, s, k/.

The Tense consonants are made with tension in the muscles throughout the vocal organs, and are the consonants /p', t', ts', s', k'/.

The Aspirated consonants are accompanied by an explosive puff of breath: /p^h, t^h, ts^h, k^h/.

Chart 4. Consonant Contrasts

Plain	ㅂ	ㄷ	ㅈ	ㅅ	ㄱ
Tense	ㅃ	ㄸ	ㅉ	ㅆ	ㄲ
Aspirated	ㅍ	ㅌ	ㅊ		ㅋ

a) ㅂ, ㅃ, ㅍ [p, p', p^h]

    비다   삐다   피다

    벼   뼈   펴

b) ㄷ, ㄸ, ㅌ [t, t', tʰ]

더   떠   터
데   떼   테

c) ㅈ, ㅉ, ㅊ [ts, ts', tsʰ]

자다   짜다   차다
지다   찌다   치다

d) ㅅ, ㅆ [s, s']

사다   싸다
시   씨

e) ㄱ, ㄲ, ㅋ [k, k', kʰ]

개다   깨다   캐다
기다   끼다   키다

Exercise 3. Practice pronouncing Plain, Tense and Aspirated Consonants.

1. 비 삐 피, 비 삐 피, 삐 피 비, 삐 피 비, 피 비 삐, 피 비 삐
   <u>브 쁘 프</u>, <u>브 쁘 프</u>, <u>쁘 프 브</u>, <u>쁘 프 브</u>, <u>프 브 쁘</u>, <u>프 브 쁘</u>
   바 빠 파, 바 빠 파, 빠 파 바, 빠 파 바, 파 바 빠, 파 바 빠

2. 디 띠 티, 디 띠 티, 띠 티 디, 띠 티 디, 티 디 띠, 티 디 띠
   드 뜨 트, 드 뜨 트, 뜨 트 드, 뜨 트 드, 트 드 뜨, 트 드 뜨
   다 따 타, 다 따 타, 따 타 다, 따 타 다, 타 다 따, 타 다 따

3. 지 찌 치, 지 찌 치, 찌 치 지, 찌 치 지, 치 지 찌, 치 지 찌
   즈 쯔 츠, 즈 쯔 츠, 쯔 츠 즈, 쯔 츠 즈, 츠 즈 쯔, 츠 즈 쯔
   자 짜 차, 자 짜 차, 짜 차 자, 짜 차 자, 차 자 짜, 차 자 짜

4. 시 씨, 시 씨, 시 씨, 씨 시, 씨 시, 씨 시
   스 쓰, 스 쓰, 스 쓰, 쓰 스, 쓰 스, 쓰 스
   사 싸, 사 싸, 사 싸, 싸 사, 싸 사, 싸 사

5. 기 끼 키, 기 끼 키, 끼 키 기, 끼 키 기, 키 기 끼,
   키 기 끼
   그 끄 크, 그 끄 크, 끄 크 그, 끄 크 그, 크 그 끄,
   크 그 끄
   가 까 카, 가 까 카, 까 카 가, 까 카 가, 카 가 까,
   카 가 까

2. Distinctions according to Place of Articulation

Consonants can be distinguished according to the place of articulation, as follows:

Sounds produced
    with both lips   are   (bi-)labials
    between the tip of the tongue and
        the alveolar ridge   are   alveolars
    between the front of the tongue
        and the palate   are   alveo-palatals
    between the back portion of the tongue
        and the velum   are   velars
    with the glottis   are   glottals

The places of articulation are shown in the chart below. (cf. Chart 4: The Consonants):

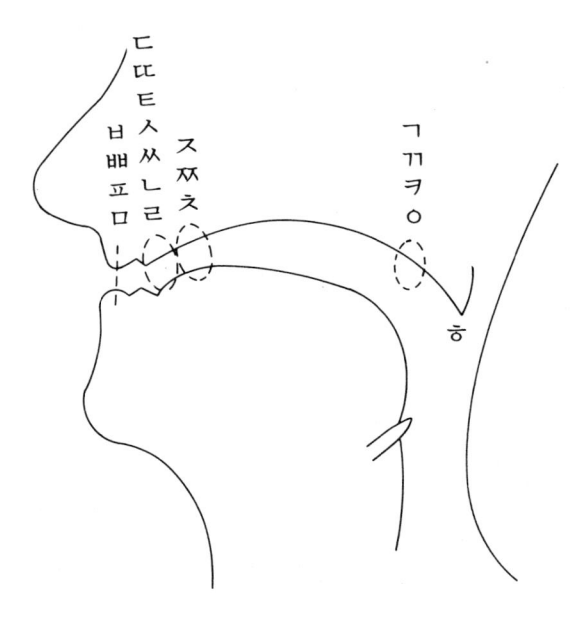

Lesson Three

Combinations of Vowel and Consonant

Given the information on tongue position and height, and also the place and manner of articulation from the preceding lessons, pronounce the consonants below in combination with vowels and then write them.

1.

Vowels Consonants	ㅏ[a] ㅑ[ja]	ㅓ[ɔ] ㅕ[jɔ]	ㅗ[o] ㅛ[jo]	ㅜ[u] ㅠ[ju]	ㅡ[ɨ] ㅣ[i]
ㄱ [k]	가 갸	거 겨	고 교	구 규	그 기
ㄱ					
ㄲ [k']	까 꺄	꺼 껴	꼬 꾜	꾸 뀨	끄 끼
ㄲ					
ㄴ [n]	나 냐	너 녀	노 뇨	누 뉴	느 니
ㄴ					
ㄷ [t]	다 댜	더 뎌	도 됴	두 듀	드 디
ㄷ					
ㄸ [t']	따 땨	떠 뗘	또 뚀	뚜 뜌	뜨 띠
ㄸ					

Exercise 4.1

| 가구 | 고기 | 야구 | 아기 | 여가 |
| 거기 | 여기 | 겨우 | 교가 | 요구 |

| 누나 | 누가 | 나 | 나가 | 누이 |
| 나이 | 어느 | 너 | 누구 | 가느냐 |

| 구두 | 기도 | 가도 | 드디어 | 더디다 |
| 도구 | 어디 | 오다 | 유도 | 다니다 |

2.

Consonants \ Vowels	ㅏ	ㅑ	ㅓ	ㅕ	ㅗ	ㅛ	ㅜ	ㅠ	ㅡ	ㅣ
ㄹ [r]	라	랴	러	려	로	료	루	류	르	리
ㄹ										
ㅁ [m]	마	먀	머	며	모	묘	무	뮤	므	미
ㅁ										
ㅂ [p]	바	뱌	버	벼	보	뵤	부	뷰	브	비
ㅂ										
ㅃ [p']	빠	뺘	뻐	뼈	뽀	뾰	뿌	쀼	쁘	삐
ㅃ										

Exercise 4.2

| 노루 | 유리 | 나라 | 요리 | 라디오 |
| 도로 | 교류 | 다리 | 거리 | 기러기 |

| 무 | 이마 | 머리 | 모두 | 너무 |
| 모기 | 무기 | 묘기 | 어머니 | 다리미 |

| 부모 | 비누 | 바보 | 두부 | 벼 |
| 바다 | 벼루 | 보리 | 보다 | 비 |

3.

Consonants \ Vowels	ㅏ	ㅑ	ㅓ	ㅕ	ㅗ	ㅛ	ㅜ	ㅠ	ㅡ	ㅣ
ㅅ [s]	사	샤	서	셔	소	쇼	수	슈	스	시
ㅅ										
ㅆ [s']	싸	쌰	써	쎠	쏘	쑈	쑤	쓔	쓰	씨
ㅆ										
ㅇ [ŋ]	아	야	어	여	오	요	우	유	으	이
ㅇ										
ㅈ [ts]	자	쟈	저	져	조	죠	주	쥬	즈	지
ㅈ										
ㅉ [ts']	짜	쨔	쩌	쪄	쪼	쬬	쭈	쮸	쯔	찌
ㅉ										

Exercise 4.3

| 수도 | 소리 | 다시 | 사다 | 소고기 |
| 시기 | 서기 | 수리 | 도시 | 소나무 |

| 아기 | 오이 | 우유 | 여기 | 이야기 |
| 나이 | 이마 | 사유 | 요사이 | 어머니 |

| 자주 | 저기 | 바지 | 부자 | 저고리 |
| 지구 | 가지 | 거지 | 그저 | 주다 |

4.

Vowels Consonants	ㅏ	ㅑ	ㅓ	ㅕ	ㅗ	ㅛ	ㅜ	ㅠ	ㅡ	ㅣ
ㅊ [tsʰ]	차	챠	처	쳐	초	쵸	추	츄	츠	치
ㅊ										
ㅋ [kʰ]	카	캬	커	켜	코	쿄	쿠	큐	크	키
ㅋ										
ㅌ [tʰ]	타	탸	터	텨	토	툐	투	튜	트	티
ㅌ										
ㅍ [pʰ]	파	퍄	퍼	펴	포	표	푸	퓨	프	피
ㅍ										
ㅎ [h]	하	햐	허	혀	호	효	후	휴	흐	히
ㅎ										

Exercise 4.4

| 차 | 마차 | 치마 | 고추 | 기차 |
| 초 | 추수 | 기초 | 차차 | 가치 |

| 코 | 크기 | 코코아 | 비키다 | 코스모스 |
| 키 | 크다 | 스키 | 시키다 | 아카시아 |

| 터 | 토지 | 타자기 | 사투리 | 터어키 |
| 티 | 로타리 | 타파 | 도토리 | 서투르다 |

| 파 | 포도 | 피리 | 피부 | 기차표 |
| 피 | 파리 | 표구 | 포로 | 아프다 |

| 휴가 | 오후 | 혀 | 후추 | 호수 |
| 하다 | 효도 | 하수구 | 흐리다 | 허수아비 |

36 / II. The Phonemes of Korean

5.

Vowels\Consonants	ㅐ [ɛ]	ㅒ [jɛ]	ㅔ [e]	ㅖ [je]	ㅘ [wa]	ㅙ [wɛ]	ㅚ [ö/we]	ㅝ [wɔ]	ㅞ [we]	ㅟ [ü/wi]	ㅢ [ɨi]
ㅇ	애	얘	에	예	와	왜	외	워	웨	위	의
ㅇ											

Lesson Three: Combinations of Vowel and Consonant / 37

Exercise 4.5

1. ㅐ
   새   개   애기   개미   어깨   매우   대우
   내   해   배우   재수   채무   후배   배추

2. ㅒ
   얘   얘기

3. ㅔ
   제자   어제   세수   네시   그게   이제
   네개   모레   시세   그네   매주   미제

4. ㅖ
   예비   예의   시계   지폐   주례   폐

5. ㅘ
   사과   기와   다과   조화   과부   미화
   화   과자   좌우   화려하다

6. ㅙ
   왜   쾌   돼지   쾌히   쐐기   유쾌하다

7. ㅚ
   사회   회화   시외   교회   죄   최소
   사퇴   후회   후퇴   의외   쇠고기   회의

8. ㅝ
   뭐   줘   둬   궈   눠   봐

9. ㅞ
   쉐터   꿰매다   궤

10. ㅟ
    위   귀   뒤   쥐   더위   추위
    뛰다 쉬다 취하다

11. ㅢ
    의사   의회   의무   거의   회의   제의
    무늬   희다   띄다   씌우다
    누구의 차   너의 자리   우리나라의 지도

Lesson Four

Syllable-Final Sounds (*patčhim*)

1. *Patčhim*

Only seven consonants may end a *pronounced* (as opposed to a written) syllable in Korean: ㄱ, ㄴ, ㄷ, ㄹ, ㅁ, ㅂ, ㅇ [k, n, t, l, m, p, ŋ]. Any other syllable-final consonants or combinations of consonants change in pronunciation to one of these seven consonants.

If the *patčhim* is followed by a particle, ending or suffix beginning with a vowel, it is pronounced (un-changed) as the *first* sound of the following syllable.

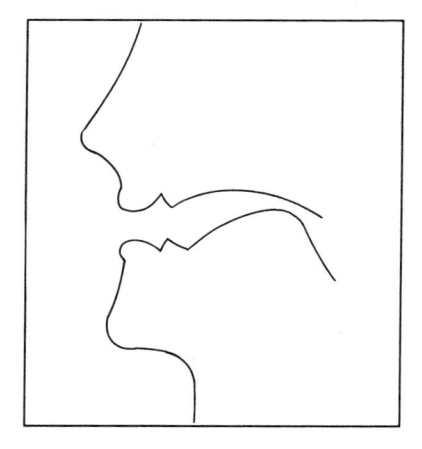

a) ㄱ, ㄲ, ㅋ → [k]

40 / II. The Phonemes of Korean

국	[국]	책	속	가족	약	취직
밖	[박]	깎다	섞다	꺾다	슦다	
부엌	[부엌]	동녘	저녁녘	새벽녘	들녘	동틀녘

When combined with a following vowel, ㄱ, ㄲ, ㅋ are pronounced [k, k', kʰ], respectively as the first sound of the following syllable.

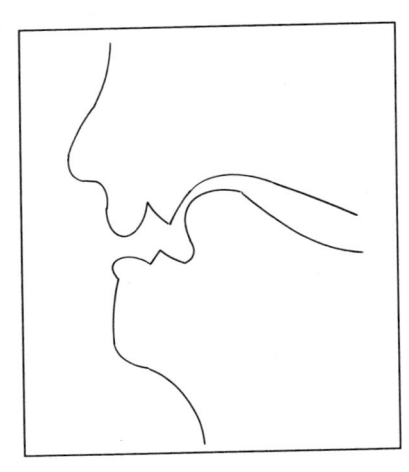

국	국에	[구게]	밖	밖에	[바께]
독	독이	[도기]	깎다	깎아서	[까까서]
책	책을	[채글]	부엌	부엌에	[부어케]
가족	가족이	[가조기]	동녘	동녘에	[동녀케]
약속	약속으로	[약소그로]	들녘	들녘으로	[들녀크로]
취직	취직을	[취지글]	저녁녘	저녁녘에	[저녁녀케]
속다	속아서	[소가서]	새벽녘	새벽녘에	[새벽녀케]

b) ㄴ → [n]

| 손 | [손] | 산 | 돈 | 문 | 신문 | 한문 |
| | | 지진 | 수건 | 준비 | 연구 | 문제 |

When combined with a following vowel, ㄴ is pronounced [n] as the first sound of the following syllable.

손	손이	[소니]
산	산에	[사네]
돈	돈을	[도늘]
문	문으로	[무느로]
인간	인간에게	[인가네게]
신문	신문에서	[신무네서]
신다	신어서	[시너서]

c) ㄷ, ㅅ, ㅆ, ㅈ, ㅊ, ㅌ, ㅎ → [t]

믿다 [믿따]	닫다	굳다	얻다	싣다
옷 [옫]	맛	낫	벗다	웃다
있다 [읻따]	갔다	왔다	썼다	샀다
낮 [낟]	잊다	늦다	맞다	젖다
낯 [낟]	꽃	빛	낯	쫓다
밭 [받]	겉	끝	밑	뱉다
낳다 [나타]	좋다	빻다	쌓다	이렇다*

*When ㅎ combines with /p,t,ts,k/, it produces /p^h, t^h, ts^h, k^h/, respectively, as the first sound of the following syllable.(see page 109)

When combined with a following vowel, ㄷ, ㅅ, ㅆ, ㅈ, ㅊ, ㅌ, ㅎ are pronounced [t, s, s', ts, ts^h, t^h, h] as the first sound of the following syllable.

믿다	믿으니	[미드니]	닫다	닫아서	[다다서]
옷	옷이	[오시]	웃다	웃어서	[우서서]
있다	있으면	[이쓰면]	갔다	갔으니까	[가쓰니까]

42 / II. The Phonemes of Korean

꽃	꽃으로 [꼬츠로]	쫓다	쫓았으나 [쪼차쓰나]
끝	끝에서 [끄테서]	뱉다	뱉으니 [배트니]
좋다	좋은 [조은]	낳다	낳아서 [나아서]*

*Between voiced sounds, ㅎ weakens or disappears.

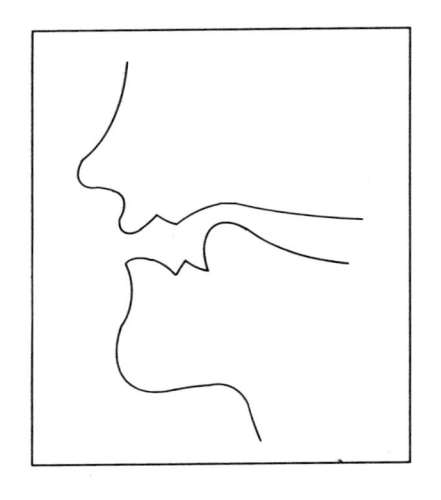

d) ㄹ → [r, l]

달 [달]　물　얼굴　팔　지하철　수술
　　　　내일　일기　길　굴비　살구

In combination with a vowel, the sound value of ㄹ is changed from [l] to [r]. That is, as a syllable-initial sound, ㄹ is pronounced [r], and as a syllable-final sound, it is pronounced [l]. When a syllable-final ㄹ combines with a particle, ending or suffix beginning with a vowel, it is pronounced [r] as the first sound of the following syllable.

달	달을	[다를]	[taril]
물	물에	[무레]	[mure]
얼굴	얼굴이	[얼구리]	[ɔlguri]

Lesson Four: Syllable-Final Sounds *(patčhim)* / 43

수술	수술을	[수수를]	[susurɨl]
팔월	팔월에	[파풔레]	[parwɔre]
지하철	지하철에는	[지하처레는]	[tsihatsʰɔrenɨn]
팔다	팔아서	[파라서]	[parasɔ]

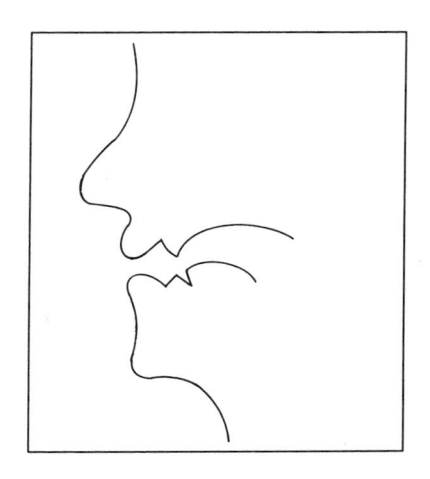

e) ㅁ → [m]

| **마음** [마음] | 감 | 봄 | 김 | 바람 | 심다 |
| | 담배 | 침대 | 남자 | 감기 | 감다 |

When combined with a following vowel, ㅁ is pronounced [m] as the first sound of the following syllable.

봄	봄에	[보메]
감	감을	[가믈]
김	김으로	[기므로]
남	남에게	[나메게]
마음	마음에	[마으메]
바람	바람이	[바라미]
심다	심어서	[시머서]

II. The Phonemes of Korean

f) ㅂ, ㅍ → [p]

집 [집]　밥　법　입구　잡지　접시　돕다
앞 [압]　숲　짚　잎　옆집　덮개　얺다

When combined with a following vowel, ㅂ, ㅍ are pronounced [p] and [pʰ] as the first sound of the following syllable.

집	집에	[지베]	앞	앞에	[아페]
밥	밥을	[바블]	숲	숲에서	[수페서]
법	법이	[버비]	잎	잎이	[이피]
삽	삽으로	[사브로]	짚	짚으로	[지프로]
일곱	일곱에서	[일고베서]	강당 옆	강당 옆에	[강당 여페]
업다	업으니까	[어브니까]	덮다	덮어	[더퍼]

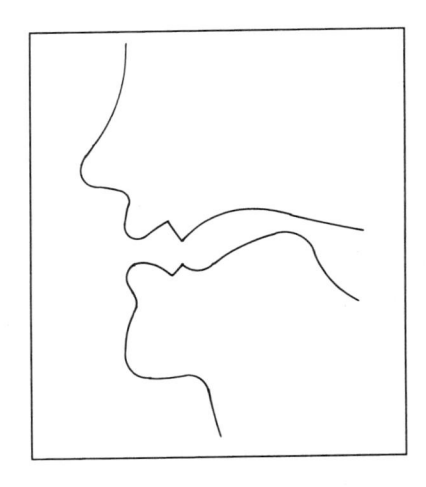

g) ㅇ → [ŋ]

강 [강]　방　강당　시장　공항　야망
　　　　당장　여성　성경　사랑방　명동

When combined with a following vowel, ㅇ is not pronounced [ŋ] as the first sound of the following syllable.

강	강에	[강에]	[kaŋe]
방	방에서	[방에서]	[paŋesɔ]
공	공으로	[공으로]	[koŋɨro]
야망	야망이	[야망이]	[jamaŋi]
시장	시장에	[시장에]	[sidzaŋe]
공항	공항으로	[공항으로]	[koŋhaŋɨro]
강당	강당은	[강당은]	[kaŋdaŋin]

Exercise 5. Reading Syllable-Final Sounds

1. 친구 집에서 저녁 밥을 먹었습니다.
   I ate supper at a friend's house.

2. 앞치마를 입고 일하세요.
   Put on an apron and work!

3. 나무 잎이 떨어집니다.
   The tree leaves are falling.

4. 차를 집 앞에 세웠습니다.
   I parked the car in front of the house.

5. 저를 믿고 따라 오세요.
   Trust me and follow along!

6. 문 좀 닫아 주세요.
   Please close the door.

7. 낫과 호미를 샀어요.
   I bought a scythe and a hoe.

8. 낫으로 풀을 벱니다.
   I'm cutting the grass with a scythe.

9. 낮과 밤의 길이가 같습니까?
   Are day and night the same in length?

10. 낮에는 온도가 높아요.
    During the day, the temperature is high.

11. 애기가 낯선 사람을 보고 울어요.
    The child cries when it sees a strange face.

12. 밭에 팥과 옥수수를 심었습니다.
    I planted red beans and corn in the fields.

13. 햇빛이 너무 뜨겁습니다.
    The sun is too hot.

14. 저는 국을 좋아합니다.
    I like soup.

15. 약속 시간이 몇 시입니까?
    What time is the appointment?

16. 동녘 땅에 가보고 싶어요.
    I want to go to the east.

17. 부엌에서 뭘 하세요?
    What are you doing in the kitchen?

18. 미역국을 잡숴 보셨어요?
    Have you ever tried seaweed soup?

19. 옷감을 사 가지고 바지를 만들려고요.
    I'm intending to buy cloth and make some trousers.

20. 언니, 산으로 올라가자.
    언니 (or 누나 older sister), let's go up the mountain.

21. 눈이 내리는군요.
    It's snowing!

22. 빵과 과일을 살까요?
    Shall I buy some bread and fruit?

23. 이 공장에서 운동기구를 만듭니다.
    We make sports equipment at this factory.

24. 일월 일일에 만납시다.
    Let's meet on January 1.

25. 바람이 솔솔 붑니다.
    The wind is blowing gently.

Exercise 6. Reading the *patčhim* "ㅇ".

1. 공부합니다.
   I'm studying.

2. 농부가 일합니다.
   The farmer is working.

3. 사랑방에서 이야기합시다.
   Let's chat in the sarangbang.

4. 홍보가 잘 되어 있습니다.
   The PR has turned out well.

5. 방법을 모르겠습니다.
   I don't know how to do it (the method).

6. 장마가 졌습니다
   The rainy season has set in.

7. 정말 재미있습니까?
   Is it truly interesting?

8. 장미가 예쁩니다.
   The roses are pretty.

9. 창문을 여십시오
   Please open the window.

10. 강물이 많아졌습니다.
    The river has risen.

11. 선생님 안녕하십니까?
    How are you?

12. 명나라가 어디에 있습니까?
    Where is the land of the Ming?

13. 형님은 방에 계십니다.
    My older brother is in his room.

14. 강남으로 이사합니다.
    We're moving to Kangnam.

15. 동남아로 갑시다.
    Let's go to Southeast Asia.

16. 공장에서 일합니다.
    I work at a factory.

17. 상자에 넣으십시오.
    Place it in the box.

18. 경주에 고적이 있습니다.
    There are historical remains in Kyŏngju.

19. 그 상점에서 사지 마십시오.
    Don't buy it from that shop!

20. 그는 성질이 아주 나쁩니다.
    His temperament is very bad.

21. 경치가 참 아름답습니다.
    The scenery is really beautiful.

22. 공책을 안 가지고 왔습니다.
    I came without my notebook.

23. 홍차가 맛이 이상합니다.
    The tea tastes strange.

24. 선생은 공처가입니까?
    Are you a hen-pecked husband?

25. 저는 상추를 좋아합니다.
    I like lettuce.

26. 방안이 춥습니다.
    It's cold in the room.

27. 공항에는 사람이 많습니다.
    There are many people at the airport.

28. 호랑이는 무서워 하지 않습니다.
    I'm not afraid of tigers.(or Tigers are not afraid.)

29. 내 입장이 곤란합니다.
    My position is difficult.

30. 오징어를 파는 상인이 부릅니다.
    The merchant selling squid is calling out.

2. Complex *patčhim*

Complex *patčhim* are reduced to one consonant at the end of a word or syllable. Some reduce to the first letter, some to the last, and some allow you to pronounce either of the constituent consonants. When these complex *patčhim* combine with a particle, ending or suffix beginning with a vowel, the last member of the complex *patčhim* is pronounced as the first sound of the following syllable.

Chart 5. **Syllable-final Consonants**

patčhim (single and double)		Complex *patčhim*		
		First Consonant	Last Consonant	Either Consonant
ㄱ	ㄱ, ㄲ, ㅋ	ㄳ		ㄺ
ㄴ	ㄴ	ㄵ, ㄶ		
ㄷ	ㄷ, ㅅ, ㅆ, ㅈ, ㅊ, ㅌ, ㅎ			
ㄹ	ㄹ	ㄽ, ㄾ, ㅀ		ㄺ, ㄼ
ㅁ	ㅁ		ㄻ	
ㅂ	ㅂ, ㅍ	ㅄ	ㄿ	ㄼ
ㅇ	ㅇ			

a) The combinations /ㄳ, ㄵ, ㄶ, ㄽ, ㄾ, ㅀ, ㅄ/ reduce to their first constituent member.

ㄳ [k]

몫	[목]	몫으로	[목스로]
삯	[삭]	삯이	[삭시]
넋	[넉]	넋을	[넉슬]

ㄵ [n]

| 앉다 | [안따] | 앉아서 | [안자서] |
| 얹다 | [언따] | 얹으니 | [언즈니] |

52 / II. The Phonemes of Korean

ㄶ [n]

많다	[만타]	많으면	[마느면]
괜찮다	[괜찬타]	괜찮아서	[괜차나서]

ㄹㅅ [l]

외곬	[외골]	외곬으로	[외골쓰로]
곬	[골]	곬에	[골쎄]

ㄹㅌ [l]

핥다	[할따]	핥아	[할타]
훑다	[훌따]	훑으니	[훌트니]

ㄹㅎ [l]

잃다	[일타]	잃어서	[이러서]
싫다	[실타]	싫으니까	[시르니까]
앓다	[알타]	앓아서	[아라서]
옳다	[올타]	옳으면	[오르면]

ㅂㅅ [p]

값	[갑]	값이	[갑씨]
없다	[업따]	없으니까	[업쓰니까]

b) The combinations /ㄻ/ and /ㄿ/ reduce to their last constituent member.

ㄹㅁ [m]

삶다	[삼따]	삶아	[살마]
젊다	[점따]	젊어서	[절머서]
굶다	[굼따]	굶으니까	[굴므니까]
옮다	[옴따]	옮으면	[올므면]

ㄿ [p]

      읊다   [읖따]   읊어   [을퍼]

c) The combinations /ㄼ/ and /ㄺ/ reduce to either of their constituent parts.

Examples where /ㄼ/ reduces to /ㄹ/:

얇다	[얄따]	얇아서	[얄바서]
넓고	[널꼬]	넓으면	[널브면]
짧게	[짤께]	짧으니까	[짤브니까]
엷다	[열따]	엷은	[열븐]
여덟	[여덜]	여덟이	[여덜비]

Examples where /ㄼ/ reduces to /ㅂ/:

밟지	[밥찌]	밟아서	[발바서]

Examples where /ㄺ/ reduces to /ㄹ/:

맑고	[말꼬]	맑으면	[말그면]
묽게	[물께]	묽어서	[물거서]
밝고	[발꼬]	밝은	[발근]
읽고	[일꼬]	읽으니까	[일그니까]

Examples where /ㄺ/ reduces to /ㄱ/:

닭	[닥]	닭이	[달기]
흙	[흑]	흙으로	[흘그로]
맑다	[막따]	맑아서	[말가서]
늙지	[늑찌]	늙으면	[늘그면]
붉다	[북따]	붉은	[불근]
읽지	[익찌]	읽으면	[일그면]

Exercise 7. Read the following sentences out loud, paying careful attention to complex *patchim*.

1. 값도 싸고 질도 좋습니다.
   The price is cheap and the quality is good.

2. 오늘은 시간이 없어요.
   Today I have no time.

3. 과일 값이 너무 올랐습니다.
   The price of fruit has gone up too much.

4. 없는 물건을 어디에서 찾습니까?
   Where do you look for things they don't have?

5. 그 아이가 넋 나간 것 같아요.
   That child seems to have lost its mind.

6. 저고리 삯과 치마 삯이 다릅니까?
   Is the charge for a vest different from the charge for a skirt?

7. 밝고 맑은 세상을 만들어야죠.
   We must build a bright, lucid world.

8. 감나무에 감이 많이 달렸습니다.
   There are many persimmons hanging from the persimmon tree.

9. 삶은 계란을 좋아합니까?
   Do you like boiled eggs?

10. 하루종일 굶고 일할 수 있습니까?
    Can you work after starving all day long?

11. 밭과 논이 많으니까 일이 많습니다.
    Since there are lots of paddies and fields, there is a lot of work.

12. 농부가 농사를 짓지 않으면 누가 짓습니까?
    If farmers don't do the farming, who will?

13. 달빛이 밝습니다.
    The moonlight is bright.

14. 외곬으로 공부해야 성공합니까?
    Does one have to follow one line of study in order to succeed?

15. 개는 핥아야 먹지 핥지 않고는 먹을 수 없나봐요.
    Dogs have to lick something before they eat it; it seems they won't eat it without licking it first.

16. 이 물건은 잃어버리면 안 됩니다.
    You mustn't lose these things.

17. 너 그 사람 싫지?
    You don't like him, do you?

18. 자리를 옮겨 앉아야 겠습니다.
    We'll have to change our seats.

19. 사과 여덟 개 사왔습니다.
    I've bought eight apples.

20. 넓고 넓은 밤 하늘이야.
    It's an ever-so-broad evening sky.

21. 닭고기하고 쇠고기를 조금 사와요.
    Please buy some chicken and some beef.

22. 맑은 물이 흘러간다.
    Clear water is flowing by.

Exercise 8. Writing as it is pronounced. In the blank spaces below, write the words above them in Han'gŭl, as they are pronounced.

1. 옆 집에 사는 아주머니가 우리 집 앞에서 꽃을 팔고 있습니다.
   ( )( )   (   )

   The lady living next door is selling flowers in front of our house.

2. 나무 잎을 모으려고 연습장 속에 넣어 두었습니다.
        (   )   (   )

   I placed it inside my exercise book thinking I would collect leaves.

3. 깊고 깊은 산 속에서 호랑이를 잡았습니다.
   ( )( )   (   )

   They caught a tiger deep in the mountains.

4. 믿는 나무에 발등 찍힌다고 너무 믿으면 안 됩니다.
   (   )   (   )

   (Since they say:) "You get branded by the tree you lean on", you shouldn't rely on him too much.

5. 예쁜 옷을 입고 다섯시에 약속 장소에 나갔습니다.
         (   )   (   )

   I put on some pretty clothes and at 5 o'clock went off to the appointed-place.

6. 늦잠을 잤는데도 낮에 또 낮잠을 잤습니다.
       (   )   (   )

   Even though I slept late, I took another nap in the afternoon.

7. 애기가 낯선 사람을 보고 낯이 설다고 웁니다.
          (   )   (   )

   Seeing an unfamiliar person, the baby cries because ["saying"] it is a strange face.

Lesson Four: Syllable-Final Sounds *(patčhim)* / 57

8. 친구가 회사를 맡아 달라고 했지만 맡지 않았습니다.
                 ( )   ( )
    My friend asked me to take care of the company, but I didn't.

9. 그는 한국에 와서 한국 가정에서 살고 있습니다.
        ( )   ( )
    He has come to Korea and is living with a Korean family.

10. 아이는 밖에서 놀다가 부엌에 계시는 어머니를 보고 부엌
          ( )   ( )   ( )
    쪽으로 달려 갔습니다.
    The child was playing outside, but when he saw his mother working in the kitchen he ran towards the kitchen.

11. 돈이 없어서 값도 물어 보지 못했습니다.
           ( )( )
    I don't have any money, so I didn't even ask the price.

12. 내 몫도 못 받았는데 여덟 사람 몫을 어떻게 받았습니까?
      ( )   ( )   ( )
    I haven't even received my share, so how did you get 8 people's worth?

13. 개가 제 새끼를 핥고 있다가 나를 훑어보더니 짖기 시작합니다.
               ( )   ( )
    The dog, licking its puppy, starts to bark after giving a searching glance at me.

14. 괜찮다고 말했는데도 가기 싫으면 싫다고 말하래요.
      ( )   ( )( )
    Even though I said "OK", he says to just say "No" if I don't want to go.

58 / II. The Phonemes of Korean

15. 벌로 손을 머리에 얹고 땅 바닥에 앉아 있었습니다.
                  ( )   ( )

    As punishment, he was sitting on the floor with his hands on his head.

16. 젊고 예쁜 아가씨가 계란을 삶아 가지고 들어왔습니다.
       ( )   ( )

    The pretty young girl boiled an egg and brought it in.

17. 달 밝은 밤에 눈을 밟고 또 밟으면서 시를 읊어 보았습니다.
         ( )   ( ) ( )   ( )

    On a bright moon-lit night, treading and re-treading the snow, I recited poetry.

18. 바지를 짧게 해 달라고 했더니 너무 짧아서 입을 수가 없습니다.
        ( )   ( )   ( )

    I asked them to shorten my trousers, but (now) they are too short to wear.

19. 굵고 낮은 목소리로 책을 읽으니까 꼭 늙은이 같습니다.
     ( )   ( )   ( )

    Since he reads the book in a coarse, low voice, he sounds just like an old man.

20. 그는 많고 많은 재산을 다 없애 버렸습니다.
          ( ) ( )   ( )

    He got rid of all his many, many possessions.

Exercise 9. Pronunciation Contrasts

1. 이 [i] and 으 [ɨ]

김	금
길	글
집	즙
기분	그분

이름	지금	기쁨	입금	기능
근심	즉시	크기	급히	승진

2. 으 [ɨ] and 어 [ɔ]

늘	널
틀	털
승격	성격
즉시	적시

그럼	근처	음성	증거	증정
어느	저금	어른	전등	전근

3. 이 [i] and 어 [ɔ]

김	검
이름	어름
지금	저금
치마	처마

직접	일어	실천	직업	기적
머리	저기	점심	성인	천지

4. 어 [ɔ] and 아 [a]

검	감

벌   발
너무   나무
컴컴하다 캄캄하다

얼마   석간   건강   정가   설탕
가정   남성   감정   참석   학업

5. 어 [ɔ] and 오 [o]

거기   고기
범   봄
넣다   놓다
덜다   돌다

서도   전보   성공   처소   전공
독서   농업   소설   조언   보전

6. 으 [ɨ] and 우 [u]

글   굴
그분   구분
근대   군대
은행   운행

무   금주   승부   능숙
문득   우측   궁금   울긋불긋

Exercise 10. Read the following sentences out loud, paying careful attention to the vowels.

1. 이 애가 내 동생입니다.
   This child is my younger brother.

2. 후배 여학생이 예쁩니다.
   The junior female student is pretty.

3. 얘기 좀 합시다.
   Let's talk a bit.

4. 애가 어디 갔지?
   Where did he go?

5. 지금 몇 시입니까?
   What time is it now?

6. 좋은 데 데리고 가십시오.
   Take her somewhere nice.

7. 폐가 많습니다.
   It's a lot of trouble.

8. 예식장에 늦게 도착했습니다.
   We arrived late at the ceremony hall.

9. 대합실에 관광객이 많습니다.
   There are many tourists in the waiting room.

10. 괜히 화를 냅니다.
    He gets angry for no reason.

11. 왜냐하면 말로 설명하기가 어렵기 때문입니다.
    It's because it's difficult to explain in words.

12. 외삼촌은 회냉면을 굉장히 좋아합니다.
    My uncle on my mother's side really likes hoenaengmyon.

13. 소원이 뭔지 말해 보십시오.
    Please tell us your wish.

14. 입원한 환자가 모두 몇 사람 입니까?
    How many patients have been admitted in total?

15. 선생님, 여기 웬일이십니까?
    Teacher, what's the matter here?

16. 웬걸요. 제가 졌습니다
    Oh, dear, I've lost!

17. 화병이 책상위에 있습니다.
    The flower vase is on the desk.

18. 의사의 지시를 따르십시오.
    Follow the doctor's orders.

19. 옥희와 영희는 성의를 다 했습니다.
    Okhi and Yŏnghi did their best.

20. 국회의원들이 회의에서 싸웠습니다.
    The Assemblymen fought at their meeting.

Exercise 11. Practice reading the contrast 에 [e] vs. 애 [ɛ].

1. 개는 좋아하지만 게를 싫어합니다.
   I like dogs but I hate crabs.

2. 베옷을 입고 배를 타고 갔습니다.
   After putting on hempen clothes, I went off in the boat.

3. 점심 때 떼를 지어 점심 먹으러 갑니다.
   At lunch time, we go off to eat lunch in groups.

4. 내일 학생 네 명을 초대했습니다.
   I've invited four students tomorrow.

5. 이 물건이 네 것이냐, 내 것이냐?
   Is this yours or mine?

6. 새해부터 세배하러 다녀야겠습니다.
   From New Year's Day I'll have to make the rounds paying my New Year's greetings.

7. 내 발에 맞는 것으로 양말 네 켤레를 샀습니다.
   I bought four pairs of socks to fit my feet.

Exercise 12. Practice pronouncing Plain, Tense and Aspirated Consonants.

1. ㅂ, ㅃ, ㅍ [p, p', pʰ]

   1) 보리빵을 팝니다.
      They sell barley bread.

   2) 빨래는 풀해서 다리십시오.
      Starch the laundry and then iron it.

   3) 팔과 발이 맞아야지, 발이 더 빠릅니다.
      Your arms and your feet have to match, but your feet are too fast.

   4) 빨강에 비해서 파랑이 너무 진합니다.
      Compared to the red, the blue is too dark.

   5) 발에 피가 나서 빨리 약을 발랐습니다.
      My foot was bleeding, so I quickly put some medication on it.

2. ㄷ, ㄸ, ㅌ [t, t', tʰ]

   1) 나무에 달린 사과를 따려고 담을 타고 올라갔습니다.
      In order to pick apples hanging from the tree, I climbed the wall to the top.

   2) 토끼 두 마리가 도토리 떨어지는 소리에 놀랐습니다.
      The two rabbits were startled at the sound of acorns falling.

   3) 내 딸이 달밤에 뜰에서 탈춤을 연습하고 있습니다.
      My daughter is practicing the mask dance in the garden on a moon-lit night.

   4) 동생은 똥똥하고 형은 뚱뚱합니다.
      My younger brother is chubby and my older brother is fat.

5) 나는 틈틈이 뜰에다 들에서 피는 꽃들을 심었습니다.
   From time to time, I re-plant flowers blooming in the fields to the garden.

3. ㅈ, ㅉ, ㅊ [ts, ts' tsʰ]

   1) 참말로 짬이 없어 잠을 못 잤습니다.
      I truly didn't have a spare moment, so I couldn't sleep.

   2) 침도 맞고 찜질도 해서 참 좋아졌습니다.
      I've had both acupuncture and a hot pack, so it's improved a lot.

   3) 냇물은 졸졸 흐르고 바닷물은 출렁거립니다.
      The water in the stream gurgles, and the ocean waves crash.

   4) 점심을 짜게 먹었는지 찬 물만 먹고 싶습니다.
      Perhaps it's because I had a salty lunch, all I want is to drink some cold water.

   5) 진짜인지 가짜인지 구별하기가 참 어렵습니다.
      It is very difficult to tell if it's the real thing or a fake.

4. ㅅ, ㅆ [s, s']

   1) 쌀을 사러 쌀가게에 가니까 쌀은 없고 싼 보리만 있었습니다.
      When I went to the rice store to buy rice, there was only cheap barley, and no rice.

   2) 시장에서 산 씨앗을 심었는데 싹이 나지 않습니다.
      I planted the seeds I had bought at the market, but the buds are not sprouting.

   3) 고래 싸움에 새우등 터집니다.

4) 솔솔 부는 봄바람이 얼마나 쌀쌀한지 모릅니다.
   The gently blowing spring breeze is so cool!

5) 싼 물건을 샀더니 금방 못 쓰게 되었습니다.
   I bought cheap goods, and they immediately turned out to be useless.

5. ㄱ, ㄲ, ㅋ [k, k', kʰ]

1) 코끼리는 코가 길어? 꼬리가 길어?
   Does the elephant have a long nose? Or a long tail?

2) 그는 꿈이 커서 큰 그릇이 될 겁니다.
   He has great dreams, so will probably become somebody great.

3) 꿈에 금을 캐서 큰 부자가 되었습니다.
   He was digging for gold in his dreams, and so became a fabulously wealthy man.

4) 김 선생을 키가 큰 김 선생이라고 부릅니다.
   They call Mr. Kim "Tall Mr. Kim".

5) 불을 자꾸 켰다 껐다 해서 고장났습니다.
   It's broken because you keep turning the light on and off.

Exercise 13. Compare and practice the *patchim* ㅁ, ㄴ, ㅇ [m, n, ŋ] below.

1. 감　간　강
   참　찬　창
   잠　잔　장

2. 잠깐　담당　궁금　건강　진심
   농촌　농담　생선　한참　안경
   단념　김장　존경　경험　장난감
   칭찬　신념　중심　감정　선생님
   공부　상담　홍분　당번　운반

Lesson Five

Voiced and Voiceless Consonants

At the beginning of an utterance, the Plain consonants /p, t, ts, k / are voiceless ([p, t, ts, k]), but when surrounded by voiced sounds (all vowels plus / m,n,ŋ,l /) they, too, become voiced and are pronounced [b, d, dz, g]. However, this automatic sound change does not affect meaning in any way.

There are also occasions when the Plain consonants do not become voiced even in a voiced environment. Thus, the Plain consonants are sometimes tensified after syllable-final / m, n, ŋ, l / (see pp. 66-71).

1. ㅂ → voiceless [p], voiced [b]
   [p]
    바다 **보**리 **부**모 **비**
   [b]
    가**방** 이**불** 두**부** 아**버**지
    담**배** 금**방** 심**방** 겸**비**
    준**비** 난**방** 헌**병** 신**부**
    공**부** 방**법** 낭**비** 양**복**
    갈**비** 일**본** 실**비** 수술**비**

Lesson Five: Voiced and Voiceless Consonants / 69

2. ㄷ → voiceless [t], voiced [d]
   [t]
       다리   **덕**   **도**구   **댁**
   [d]
       지**도**   아**들**   구**두**   어**디**
       담**당**   침**대**   감**당**   남**대**문
       만**두**   군**대**   온**돌**   운**동**
       명**동**   경**대**   응**답**   강**당**
       돌**담**   알**다**   놀**다**   돌**다**리

3. ㅈ → voiceless [ts], voiced [dz]
   [ts]
       자꾸   **저**것   **주**인   **지**리
   [dz]
       이**제**   모**자**   바**지**   수**저**
       감**자**   남**자**   감**정**   금**지**
       진**지**   먼**지**   문**장**   안**주**
       공**장**   농**장**   창**저**   긍**지**
       글**짓**기   딸**자**식   칠**주**의   불**조**심

4. ㄱ → voiceless [k], voiced [g]
   [k]
       고기   **구**두   **거**지   **그**림
   [g]
       아**기**   누**구**   휴**가**   사**과**
       감**기**   임**금**   감**격**   금**강**산
       연**구**   친**구**   한**국**   건**강**
       정**구**   공**기**   항**구**   중**국**
       일**기**   달**걀**   물**건**   얼**굴**

Exercise 14. Taking into account the sentence position of the underlined syllables below, write whether the consonant is to be pronounced as voiced or voiceless.

E.g. 바<u>가</u>지
(v-less)

1. <u>부</u>모님께서는 일요일에 보통 집에 계십니다.
   My parents are usually at home on Sunday.

   동생은 학교에 갈 준<u>비</u>를 하느라고 책들을 가<u>방</u>에 넣고 있습니다.
   My little brother is placing his books in his bookbag as part of his preparations to go to school.

   <u>비</u>가 오니까 집에서 공<u>부</u>나 해야겠습니다.
   It's raining, so I'll have to stay at home and study or something.

   부모님   준비   가방   비가   공부
   (   )   (   )   (   )   (   )   (   )

2. 명<u>동</u>에서 구<u>두</u>를 하나 샀습니다.
   I bought a pair of shoes in Myongdong.

   <u>독</u>감에 걸려서 내과 담<u>당</u> 의사를 찾아갔습니다.
   I caught the flu, so went to see the Head of Internal Medicine.

   <u>다</u>음 달에 고향으로 돌아가려고 합니다.
   I'm intending to go back to my hometown next month.

   명동   구두   독감   담당   다음 달
   (   )   (   )   (   )   (   )   (   )

   돌아가려고
   (   )

Lesson Five: Voiced and Voiceless Consonants / 71

3. 주인 아저씨가 공장장이에요.
   The head of the house is a factory boss.

   요즘 불이 자주 나니까 불조심 해야 해요.
   Lately there have been a lot of fires so you should be careful with fire.

   저것 좀 봐요.
   Look at that!

   주인   아저씨   공장장   불조심   저것
   (   )   (   )   (   )   (   )   (   )

4. 누가 벽에다 그림을 그렸지?
   Who drew a picture on the wall?

   저는 학교 과학실에서 연구하고 있습니다.
   I am doing research in the school science room.

   나는 국군 아저씨에게 내가 쓴 일기를 보냈습니다.
   I sent the diary I wrote to a man in the Korean Army.

   누가   그렸지?   연구하고   국군   일기
   (   )   (   )   (   )   (   )   (   )

III.
Phonological Changes

Depending on the sounds either preceding or following them, sounds can undergo different kinds of phonological changes.

Lesson Six

Vowel Harmony

"Vowel Harmony" is the phenomenon whereby *yangsŏng* ("Bright") vowels (ㅏ and ㅗ) go together with following *yangsŏng* vowels, and *ŭmsŏng* ("Dark") vowels (ㅓ, ㅜ, ㅡ, ㅣ, ㅚ, ㅟ) go together with following *ŭmsŏng* vowels. The quality of a following vowel is determined depending on whether the preceding vowel belongs to the *yangsŏng* or *ŭmsŏng* set, most often in expressive vocabulary (mimetic or onomatopoeic words) and in the "infinitive" of verb endings (the -아 / -어 of Polite Sytle -아요, -어요, Past -았- / -었-, etc.).

Chart 6. **Vowel Harmony**

	Preceding Vowel	Following Vowel
Yangsŏng Vowel	ㅏ ㅗ	ㅏ
Ŭmsŏng Vowel	ㅓ ㅜ ㅡ ㅣ ㅚ ㅟ	ㅓ

Examples: 살랑살랑 : 설렁설렁
           소곤소곤 : 수근수근
           졸졸   : 줄줄
           파랗다 : 퍼렇다

1. *Yangsŏng* Vowels

a) ㅏ + ㅏ

잡다 → 잡 + 아요 → 잡아요
닫다 → 닫 + 았다 → 닫았다
같다 → 같 + 아서 → 같아서
찾다 → 찾 + 아도 → 찾아도
깎다 → 깎 + 아야 → 깎아야

b) ㅗ + ㅏ

보다 → 보 + 아요 → 보아요
놓다 → 놓 + 았다 → 놓았다
좁다 → 좁 + 아서 → 좁아서
쏟다 → 쏟 + 아도 → 쏟아도
뽑다 → 뽑 + 아야 → 뽑아야

2. *Ŭmsŏng* Vowels

a) ㅓ + ㅓ

먹다 → 먹 + 어요 → 먹어요
업다 → 업 + 었다 → 업었다
걸다 → 걸 + 어서 → 걸어서
넣다 → 넣 + 어도 → 넣어도
꺾다 → 꺾 + 어야 → 꺾어야

Lesson Six: Vowel Harmony / 77

b) ㅜ + ㅓ
　묻다　　→ 묻　　+ 어요 → 묻어요
　다투다　→ 다투　+ 었다 → 다투었다
　나누다　→ 나누　+ 어서 → 나누어서
　다루다　→ 다루　+ 어도 → 다루어도
　그만두다 → 그만두 + 어야 → 그만두어야

c) ㅡ + ㅓ
　쓰다　→ 쓰　+ 어요 → 쓰어요　→ 써요 *1
　끊다　→ 끊　+ 었다 → 끊었다
　늦다　→ 늦　+ 어서 → 늦어서
　끓다　→ 끓　+ 어도 → 끓어도
　들다　→ 들　+ 어야 → 들어야

d) ㅣ + ㅓ
　신다　　→ 신　　+ 었다 → 신었다
　믿다　　→ 믿　　+ 어서 → 믿어서
　가르치다 → 가르치 + 어도 → 가르치어도 → 가르쳐도*2
　이기다　→ 이기　+ 어야 → 이기어야　→ 이겨야

e) ㅚ + ㅓ
　괴다 → 괴 + 었다 → 괴었다
　되다 → 되 + 어서 → 되어서

f) ㅟ + ㅓ
　쉬다 → 쉬 + 어요 → 쉬어요
　쥐다 → 쥐 + 어도 → 쥐어도

*1 (see p. 56)
 2 (see p. 55)

Exercise 15. Select the correct alternative from the forms in parentheses.

1. 너무 피곤하니까 쉬(았, 었)다가 할까?
   I'm so tired; shall we rest a bit and then continue?

2. 늦(았, 었)으니까 빨리 먹(아, 어).
   It's late; hurry up and eat!

3. 담배를 피(와, 워)서 그런지 건강이 나빠졌다.
   It's probably because I smoke, but my health has deteriorated.

4. 너무 추(와, 워)서 창문을 닫(았, 었)다.
   It was too cold, so I closed the window.

5. 치마가 길(아, 어)서 줄여서 입(았, 었)다.
   The skirt was too long, so I shortened it before wearing it.

6. 이 아이는 과일을 깎(아, 어) 주(아, 어)도 울(아, 어)요.
   This kid cries even when I cut fruit for him.

7. 걸(아, 어)서 오면 늦을 것 같(아, 어)서 택시를 잡(아, 어) 탔다.
   It looked like we'd be late if we came on foot so we caught a taxi.

8. 그 사람을 한번 만나 보(았, 었)는데 믿(아, 어)도 될까?
   I met him once; do you suppose she's trustworthy?

9. 그 길은 너무 좁(아, 어)서 차가 들어가기가 어려(왔, 웠)다.
   The road was too narrow, so the car had difficulty entering.

10. 책상 위에 놓(아, 어)둔 책이 아무리 찾(아, 어)도 없다.
    No matter how hard I look, I can't find the books I put on top of the desk.

Lesson Seven

Contraction and Loss

Contraction occurs when two syllables come together and are pronounced as one. Loss occurs when one of two contiguous syllables disappears. According to the type of verb stem, there are cases of *obligatory* contraction and loss and of *optional* contraction and loss.

1. Contraction

When a preceding ㅗ meets a following ㅏ, this contracts to ㅘ
ㅜ　　　　　　　ㅓ　　　　　ㅝ
ㅣ　　　　　　　ㅓ　　　　　ㅕ
ㅣ　　　　　　　ㅗ　　　　　ㅛ

Chart 7. **Contractions**

Preceding Vowel	Following Vowel	Contraction
ㅗ	ㅏ	ㅘ
ㅜ	ㅓ	ㅝ
ㅣ	ㅓ	ㅕ
ㅣ	ㅗ	ㅛ

III. Phonological Changes

a) ㅗ + ㅏ → ㅘ

오다 → 오 + 았다 → 오았다 → <u>왔다</u> (obligatory)
보다 → 보 + 아 → <u>보아</u> → <u>봐</u> (optional)
고다 → 고 + 아서 → <u>고아서</u> → <u>과서</u> (optional)
꼬다 → 꼬 + 아도 → <u>꼬아도</u> → <u>꽈도</u> (optional)
쏘다 → 쏘 + 아야 → <u>쏘아야</u> → <u>쏴야</u> (optional)
쪼다 → 쪼 + 아야 → <u>쪼아야</u> → <u>쫘야</u> (optional)

b) ㅜ + ㅓ → ㅝ

주다 → 주 + 었다 → <u>주었다</u> → <u>줬다</u>
(optional)

배우다 → 배우 + 어 → 배우어 → <u>배워</u>
(obligatory)

외우다 → 외우 + 어서 → 외우어서 → <u>외워서</u>
(obligatory)

피우다 → 피우 + 어도 → 피우어도 → <u>피워도</u>
(obligatory)

싸우다 → 싸우 + 어야 → 싸우어야 → <u>싸워야</u>
(obligatory)

그만두다 → 그만두 + 어서 → <u>그만두어서</u> → <u>그만둬서</u>
(optional)

c) ㅣ + ㅓ → ㅕ

하시다 → 하시 + 었다 → <u>하시었다</u> → <u>하셨다</u>
(optional)

고치다 → 고치 + 어 → <u>고치어</u> → <u>고쳐</u>
(obligatory)

아끼다 → 아끼 + 어서 → <u>아끼어서</u> → <u>아껴서</u>
(obligatory)

가르치다 → 가르치 + 어도 → 가르치어도 → <u>가르쳐도</u>
  (obligatory)

기다리다 → 기다리 + 어야 → 기다리어야 → <u>기다려야</u>
  (obligatory)

꾸미다 → 꾸미 + 었다 → 꾸미었다 → <u>꾸몄다</u>
  (obligatory)

다리다 → 다리 + 어 → 다리어 → <u>다려</u>
  (obligatory)

가리다 → 가리 + 어서 → 가리어서 → <u>가려서</u>
  (obligatory)

끼치다 → 끼치 + 어도 → 끼치어도 → <u>끼쳐도</u>
  (obligatory)

d) ㅣ + ㅗ → ㅛ

아니 + 오 → <u>아니오</u> → <u>아뇨</u> (optional)

가시 + 오 → <u>가시오</u> → <u>가쇼</u> (optional)

2. Loss

When a preceding ㅏ meets a following ㅏ, the ㅏ is lost.
　　　　　　　　ㅓ　　　　　　　　ㅓ　　ㅓ
　　　　　　　　ㅡ　　　　　　　　ㅓ　　ㅡ
　　　　　　　　ㅣ　　　　　　　　ㅏ　　ㅣ

Chart 8. **Loss**

Preceding Vowel	Following Vowel	Loss
ㅏ	ㅏ	ㅏ
ㅓ	ㅓ	ㅓ
ㅡ	ㅓ	ㅡ
ㅣ	ㅏ	ㅣ

a) ㅏ + ㅏ → ㅏ
  가다 → 가 + 았다 → 가았다 → <u>갔다</u>
  (obligatory)
  사다 → 사 + 아서 → 사아서 → <u>사서</u>
  (obligatory)
  자다 → 자 + 아도 → 자아도 → <u>자도</u>
  (obligatory)
  싸다 → 싸 + 아야 → 싸아야 → <u>싸야</u>
  (obligatory)
  만나다 → 만나 + 아 보니 → 만나아 보니 → <u>만나 보니</u>
  (obligatory)

b) ㅓ + ㅓ → ㅓ
  서다 → 서 + 었다 → 서었다 → <u>섰다</u>
  (obligatory)
  건너다 → 건너 + 어서 → 건너어서 → <u>건너서</u>
  (obligatory)
  켜다 → 켜 + 어도 → 켜어도 → <u>켜도</u>
  (obligatory)
  펴다 → 펴 + 어야 → 펴어야 → <u>펴야</u>
  (obligatory)
  지내다 → 지내 + 어 보니 → <u>지내어 보니</u> → <u>지내 보니</u>
  (optional)

c) ㅡ + ㅓ → ㅓ
  쓰다 → 쓰 + 었다 → 쓰었다 → <u>썼다</u>
  (obligatory)
  크다 → 크 + 어서 → 크어서 → <u>커서</u>
  (obligatory)
  뜨다 → 뜨 + 어도 → 뜨어도 → <u>떠도</u>
  (obligatory)

끄다 → 끄 + 어야 → 끄어야 → 꺼야
(obligatory)

기쁘다 → 기쁘 + 어하다 → 기쁘어하다 → 기뻐하다
(obligatory)

d) ㅣ + ㅏ → ㅏ

크지 않다 → 크잖다 (optional)
그러지 않아도 → 그러잖아도 (optional)
할 수 없지 않아요 → 할 수 없잖아요 (optional)

Exercise 16. Fill in the underlined portions with the appropriate form, after application of contraction or loss.

E.g. 학교에 <u>갔다가</u> 우체국에 들렀습니다. (가았다가)

1. 그분이 우리 집에 _____ 갔습니다. (오았다가)
   That person dropped in at our house.

2. 그 영화는 여러번 _____ 재미있습니다. (보아도)
   No matter how many times I watch that film, it is still interesting.

3. 오늘은 시를 _____ 주셨습니다. (가르치어)
   Today she taught us poetry.

4. 선생님이 내 발음을 _____ 주셨습니다. (고치어)
   The teacher corrected my pronunciation.

5. 너무 많이 _____ . (배우었습니다)
   You've learned too much.

6. 날마다 _____ 자꾸 잊어 버립니다. (외우어도)
   Even though I memorize every day, I keep forgetting.

7. 그 옷이 너무 _____? (크지 않아요)
   Aren't those clothes too big?

8. 공부하고 싶은데 돈이 _____? (없지 않아요)
   I want to study, but I have no money!

9. 이 일을 언제 _____? (끝내지요)
   When will we finish this work, I wonder?

10. 무엇이든지 _____ _____. (아끼어서, 써야지요)
    No matter what they are, one should use things sparingly.

11. 그 사람을 사무실에 _____ 만나 봐요. (가아서)
    Go to her office and meet her!

12. 잠을 많이 _____ 또 졸려요. (자아도)
    No matter how much I sleep, I'm still sleepy.

13. 이 길을 _____ 가세요. (건너어서)
    Cross this road.

14. 너무 _____ 밥도 못 먹었어요. (바쁘어서)
    I was so busy, I couldn't even eat.

Lesson Eight

Consonant Assimilations

When a syllable-final consonant comes into contact with the initial consonant of a following syllable, the following kinds of assimilation can occur:

a) one or the other of the two consonants changes in the direction of the other, coming to resemble it in pronunciation,

b) both sounds change.

Chart 9. **Consonant Assimilation**

ㅂ ㄷ ㄱ	before	ㅁ ㄴ	become	ㅁ ㄴ ㅇ
ㄹ	after	ㅁ ㅇ ㅂ ㄷ ㄱ ㄴ	becomes	ㄴ
ㄴ	before & after	ㄹ	becomes	ㄹ

Lesson Eight: Consonant Assimilations

1. /p, t, k + m, n/ →[m, n, ŋ + m, n]

Before the nasals ㅁ/m/ and ㄴ/n/, the plosives ㅂ, ㄷ, ㄱ/p, t, k/ assimilate to ㅁ, ㄴ, ㅇ [m, n, ŋ] respectively. That is, ㅂ, ㄷ, ㄱ/p, t, k/ keep their *place* of articulation, but change their *manner* of articulation, from plosive to nasal.

a) ㅂ becomes ㅁ before the nasals ㅁ, ㄴ

E.g. **입맛** [임맏]
옵니다 [옴니다]

십만	밥물	밥맛	앞문	입문
잎마다	집만	값만	숲 밑	업무
집집마다	앞마당	밥 먹는다	값 매기다	

겹눈	읍내	덥니	앞날	잡는
깊니	없니	읊니	집는다	없는
밟는데	합니다	밥 냄비	높낮이	

b) ㄷ becomes ㄴ before the nasals ㅁ, ㄴ

E.g. **맏** **며**느리 [만 며느리]
믿는다 [민는다]

낮마다	낯만	꽃만	빛만	낱말
곳곳마다	밭만	멋만	볕만	뜻만
옷 맵시	꽃망울	옷 맞추다		

끝내	벗니	찾니	있는	못나다
꽃나무	맡니	갔니	빛난	끝나다
낯 놓고	노랗니	싣나	빗나가다	쫓는다

c) ㄱ becomes ㅇ before the nasals ㅁ, ㄴ

E.g. **백만** [뱅만]
  백년 [뱅년]

작문	밖만	한국말	곡목	영국 문화
국물	약물	국민학교	학문	교육 문제
박물관	식물	악마	식목일	부엌문
흙만	흙 말리다			

백년	작년	국내	숙녀	긁는
학년	깎는다	함박눈	낙농	책 넣는다
낚는다				

2. /m, ŋ + l/ → [m, ŋ + n]

After the nasals ㅁ and ㅇ, ㄹ becomes ㄴ.

E.g. **음력** [음녁]
  종로 [종노]

| 금리 | 침략 | 함락 | 심리학 | 담력 |
| 감리교 | 점령 | 침례교 | 참례하다 | |

궁리	공로	양력	행렬	항로
장로교	승리	장래	장려하다	대통령
정력	정류장	종류	정리하다	상륙
강릉	중력	양로원	경로석	정립

3. /p, k + l/ → [p, k + n] → [m, ŋ + n]

After ㅂ and ㄱ, ㄹ becomes ㄴ.
The [ㄴ] is resulted from this, in turn, forces preceding /ㅂ, ㄱ/ to change to [ㅁ, ㅇ].

E.g. 십리 → 십니 → [심니]
　　　백리 → 백니 → [뱅니]

| 협력 | 법률 | 압력 | 수업료 | 급료 |
| 합리적 | 섭리 | 입력 | 합류 | 답례 |

독립	국립	격려	속리산	식량
착륙	국력	목련	목례	학력
목록	박람회	박력	숙련	식료품

4. /n + l/ → [n + n]

ㄹ after ㄴ changes to ㄴ.

E.g. 판**단력** [판단녁]

| 결단력 | 이원론 | 음운론 | 신문로 | 공권력 |
| 임진란 | 생산량 | 동원령 | 입원료 | 횡단로 |

5. /n + l, l + n/ → [l + l, l + l]

ㄴ before and after ㄹ changes to ㄹ.

E.g. **천리** [철리]
　　　일년 [일련]

| 신라 | 인류 | 본론 | 연락하다 | 진리 |

논리	난로	난리	편리하다	만리장성
권력	인력	관리	권리	민란
열넷	실내	돌 날	달 나라	설날
칠년	칼날	물 난리	들 나물	팔년
줄 넘기	할는지	닳네	뚫는	핥네

Exercise 17. Read the following sentences out loud, paying careful attention to consonant assimilations.

1. 반찬이 없으니까 **밥맛**이 안 생겨요.
   There aren't any side dishes, so I have no appetite.

2. **옆 문**으로 들어가지 말고 **앞 문**으로 들어갑시다.
   Let's enter by the front door rather than by the side door.

3. **앞날**이 창창한 젊은이들을 잘 지도해 주십시오.
   Please guide these young people with bright futures well.

4. 봄이 되니까 곳**곳마**다 개나리가 한창입니다.
   Now that it's spring, the *kaenari* are in full bloom everywhere.

5. **박물**관에 가면 희귀한 물건이 많습니다.
   If you go to the museum, there are lots of rare things.

6. 장마 때문에 농**작물**의 피해가 대단합니다.
   The damage to crops because of the rains is awful.

7. 이 일은 20분이면 **넉넉**히 할 수 있습니다.
   Twenty minutes is plenty to do this job.

8. **숙녀**가 맨발로 어디에 나가?
   Where does the lady think she's going in bare feet?

9. **국민** 모두가 힘을 합하면 잘 살 수 있습니다.
   If all the people join forces, they can live well.

10. **있는** 힘을 다 해 보세요.
    Do it with all your strength!

11. 이 일을 끝내려면 앞으로 **백년**은 더 걸릴겁니다.
    If you want to finish this work, it'll take another 100 years.

12. 한국의 명절은 **음력**과 관계가 있습니다.
    Korean holidays are connected with the lunar calendar.

13. 이 학교 **창립**일은 언제입니까?
    When is this school's Founders' Day?

14. **염려**해 주신 덕분에 건강합니다.
    Thanks to your concern, I am healthy.

15. 이사를 했으면 동회에 가서 이주 **등록**을 해야 합니다.
    If you've moved, you have to go to the Tong Council and register your change of residence.

16. **심리**학을 공부했으니 남의 **심리**는 잘 아시겠군요.
    Since you've studied psychology, you must understand others' psychologies well!

17. 작은 비행기일 수록 **착륙**할 때 많이 흔들립니다.
    The smaller the plane, the more it shakes during landing.

18. **법률**에 관해 낫 놓고 기역자도 모릅니다.
    I'm totally ignorant about the law.

19. 한 시간에 **몇리**나 걸을 수 있습니까?
    How many *li* can you walk in an hour?

20. **국립**묘지는 어디로 해서 갑니까?
    How do you get to the National Cemetery?

21. 영수한테 **연락**을 하고 싶었는데 주소와 전화번호를 몰라서 하지 못했습니다.
    I wanted to contact Yŏngsu, but I didn't know his address and telephone number, so I couldn't.

22. **한라**산 꼭대기에 올라가 보았니?
    Have you ever gone to the top of Mt. Halla?

23. **한류**와 **난류**가 만나는 곳에 고기들이 많습니다.
    At the place where the cold current meets the warm current there are lots of fish.

24. 사회 질서가 점점 **혼란**해집니다.
    Social order is getting more and more chaotic.

25. **실내**에서는 금연입니다.
    No smoking indoors.

26. 제 동생은 **열네**살입니다.
    My younger sister is 14.

27. 열살쯤 되면 옳고 그른 것에 대한 판**단력**이 생깁니다.
    Once one reaches age 10 or so, one develops the judgment between right and wrong.

28. 특히 어려운 일에 부닥쳤을 때 결**단력**이 필요합니다.
    One needs determination especially when encountering difficulties.

Exercise 18. Read the following sentences out loud, then fill in the blanks with the appropriate form *as actually pronounced.*

1. 십만원만 주십시오.
   (   )
   Please give me 100,000 wŏn.

2. 날씨가 더우니까 입맛이 없어요.
                  (   )
   It's hot, so I have no appetite.

3. 옷 모양을 어떻게 할까요?
   (   )
   How shall I design the clothes ('shape)?

4. 꽃나무에 날마다 물을 주고 있니?
   (   )   (   )
   Are you watering the flowering plant every day?

5. 작년에 국민학교를 졸업했습니다.
   (   ) (   )
   I graduated from elementary school last year.

6. 냄새가 나니까 부엌 문을 열고 볶는게 어때?
                        (   )
   It smells, so how about roasting them with the kitchen door open?

7. 종로 서점에서 심리학 책을 한 권 샀습니다.
   (   )   (   )
   I bought a psychology book at Chongno Bookstore.

8. 설을 양력으로도 쇠고 음력으로도 쉽니다.
          (   )   (   )
   We celebrate New Year's Day according to both the lunar calendar and the Western calendar.

9. 십리도 못 가서 발병난다.
   (   )
   He doesn't even go 10 *li* before getting sore feet.

10. 독립문이 어디에 있습니까?
    (   )   (   )
    Where is Independence Gate?

11. 전 일년 전에 여기에 왔어요.
        (   )
    I came here one year ago.

12. 훽스가 있어서 연락하기가 편해요.
                 (   )
    I have a fax, so it's convenient for getting in touch.

13. 이 일을 성공시키기까지 결단력이 필요했어요.
                    (   )
    We needed determination to see this job through successfully.

14. 그 아이의 판단력으로는 부족합니다.
          (   )
    In that child's judgement, it's not enough.

15. 대학 시절에 음운론을 배웠는데 다 잊었습니다.
            (   )
    I studied phonology in my university days, but I've forgotten it all.

Lesson Nine

Tensification and Voicing

When two voiceless sounds come together, the second of them is tensified (ㅃ, ㄸ, ㅉ, ㅆ, ㄲ). When a voiceless and a voiced sound come together, in some cases tensification occurs, in others, voicing.

1. When voiceless sounds meet

After ㅂ, ㄷ and ㄱ, the voiceless consonants ㅂ, ㄷ, ㅈ, ㅅ, ㄱ are tensified, becoming ㅃ, ㄸ, ㅉ, ㅆ, ㄲ.

Chart 10. **Tensification**

		ㅂ	→	ㅃ
ㅂ		ㄷ	→	ㄸ
ㄷ	+	ㅈ	→	ㅉ
ㄱ		ㅅ	→	ㅆ
		ㄱ	→	ㄲ

a) ㅂ, ㄷ, ㅈ, ㅅ, ㄱ after ㅂ become ㅃ, ㄸ, ㅉ, ㅆ, ㄲ

    십분 [십뿐, 시뿐]
    법대 [법때]
    답장 [답짱]
    밥상 [밥쌍]
    입국 [입꾹]

Lesson Nine: Tensification and Voicing / 97

잡비	입법	압박	핍박	입버릇
입대	잡담	접대	답답하다	합당하다
잡지	입장	십자가	겁쟁이	값지다
답사	접시	엽서	삽시간	흡수하다
높고	깊게	잡곡	합계	덮개

b) ㅂ, ㄷ, ㅈ, ㅅ, ㄱ after ㄷ become ㅃ, ㄸ, ㅉ, ㅆ, ㄲ

돋보기 [돋뽀기, 도뽀기]
믿다 [믿따, 미따]
걷자 [걷짜, 거짜]
맏사위 [맏싸위, 마싸위]
듣고 [듣꼬, 드꼬]

늦봄	꽃밭	밑바닥	늦바람	돌솥밥
다섯달	잊도록	있던 것	늦도록	꽃다발
빗자루	늦지	곧장	잊지 마	싣자
덧신	몇시	웃사람	꽃송이	낯설다
겉과	쫓고	보았고	옷걸이	옷고름

c) ㅂ, ㄷ, ㅈ, ㅅ, ㄱ after ㄱ become ㅃ, ㄸ, ㅉ, ㅆ, ㄲ

백반 [백빤]
식당 [식땅]
학자 [학짜]
학생 [학쌩]
학교 [학꾜, 하꾜]

국밥	석방	한식부	학부모	각별히	학비	박봉
복도	속담	깍두기	목도리	넉달	낙담	확대
국제	맥주	낙제	걱정	특징	직접	식장

국수   욕심   책상   각사람   역사   목소리   약속
국군   독감   각국   떡국   목거리   악기   축구

2. When voiceless consonants meet voiced consonants

After the voiced consonants ㅁ, ㄴ, ㅇ and ㄹ, the voiceless consonants ㅂ, ㄷ, ㅈ, and ㄱ become voiced: [b, d, dz, g]. In some cases (usually after verb stems ending in -ㅁ or -ㄴ, or in compound nouns), ㅂ, ㄷ, ㅈ, ㅅ and ㄱ become tensified: ㅃ, ㄸ, ㅉ, ㅆ, ㄲ.

Chart 11. Voicing and Tensification

ㅂ			ㅂ [b] / ㅃ [p']
ㄷ		ㅁ	ㄷ [d] / ㄸ [t']
ㅈ	after	ㄴ	ㅈ [dz] / ㅉ [ts']
ㅅ		ㅇ	_____ / ㅆ [s']
ㄱ		ㄹ	ㄱ [g] / ㄲ [k']

a) ㅂ, ㄷ, ㅈ, ㅅ and ㄱ after ㅁ become

voiced [b, d, dz, g]

담배 [담배]
침대 [침대]
감자 [감자]
감기 [감기]

겹비   금방   심방   몸부림   냄비   삼베
담당   남대문   감당   담대   험담   경험담
김장   남자   몸조심   점쟁이   감정   심장
임금   침구   감격   금강산   감기다 옮기다

Lesson Nine: Tensification and Voicing / 99

    tense **[p', t', ts', s', k']**

        남빛 [남삗]
        심다 [심따]
        염증 [염쯩]
        점수 [점쑤]
        곰국 [곰꾹]

심보	봄볕	밤비	춤 바람	아침 밥
참다	숨다	젊다	좀도둑	그믐달
밤중	몸종	힘줄	심자	젊지
짐속	짐 삯	섬 사람	꿈 속에서	
엄격	숨결	염가	밤길	바람결

b) ㅂ, ㄷ, ㅈ, ㅅ and ㄱ after ㄴ become

    voiced **[b, d, dz, g]**

        신발 [신발]
        만두 [만두]
        진지 [진지]
        인구 [인구]

준비	전보	건넌방	문방구	간 밤
언덕	운동	군대	온돌	현대인
인정	간장	문제	단잠	존재하다
연구	한국	친구	건강	안기다

    tense **[p', t', ts', s', k']**

        문법 [문뻡]
        신다 [신따]
        한자 [한짜]

III. Phonological Changes

산새 [산쌔]
인격 [인껵]

안방	산불	헌법	신바람	눈병
돈독	논둑	문득	손등	앉다
문자	단점	찬장	인적자원	손 재주
산속	판소리	손수건	촌사람	앉소
안과	윤기	인기	신고	손가락

c) ㅂ, ㄷ, ㅈ, ㅅ, ㄱ after ㅇ become

voiced **[b, d, dz, g]**

공부 [공부]
명동 [명동]
공장 [공장]
공기 [공기]

쟁반	농부	사랑방	공부하다	승부
경대	응답	강당	낭독	평등
경제	농장	성적	송장	경쟁하다
정구	성경	장가	중국	경기

tense **[p', t', ts', s', k']**

등불 [등뿔]
용돈 [용똔]
빵집 [빵찝]
방세 [방쎄]
강가 [강까]

| 상보 | 방 바닥 | 강 바람 | 방비 | 등불 |
| 장대 | 공돈 | 상 다리 | 장독대 | 초승달 |

Lesson Nine: Tensification and Voicing / 101

맹점	냉증	영장	장점	상장
강속	창살	등수	종소리	창살
냉국	성격	장국밥	장기자랑	성과

d) ㅂ, ㄷ, ㅈ, ㅅ, ㄱ after ㄹ become

  voiced [b, d, dz, g]

  갈비 [갈비]
  알다 [알다]
  알지 [알지]
  일기 [일기]

질병	찰밥	절벽	일방적	굴비
돌다리	발돋움	갈도록	알더군	돌다
딸자식	글짓기	불조심	물장난	갈자
달걀	물건	얼굴	질그릇	결과

  tense [p', t', ts' s', k']

  들보 [들뽀]
  발달 [발딸]
  글자 [글짜]
  걸상 [걸쌍]
  굴국 [굴꾹]

일복	달밤	이불보	달빛	할 바를
일등	물독	갈등	절대로	핥다
실제	발전	열중	결정	할 적에
굴속	실수	물수건	일상생활	만날 사람
갈길	얼굴값	헐값	발가락	할 것을

102 / III. Phonological Changes

Exercise 19. Read the following sentences out loud.
(- for Voicing, = for Tensification)

1. 한식부에서 불고기 백반과 비빔밥을 준비했다.
   In the Korean food section they prepared *pibimpap* and *pulgoki* set meals.

2. 그날 밤 열시 이십분에 일부러 그를 찾아갔다.
   I called on him on purpose that night at 10:20.

3. 백번 듣는 것보다 한번 보는 것이 낫다.
   Seeing once is better than hearing a 100 times.

4. 학부모들이 손님들을 접대하려고 한복을 입고 꽃다발을 들고 있다.
   The school parents are wearing hanbok and holding bouquets of flowers in order to receive the guests.

5. 몇 달 동안 군대에서, 용돈을 쓸 기회가 없어서 많이 저축했다.
   I have saved up a lot during several months in the Army, as there are no opportunities to spend pocket money.

6. 한 달에 한번 아버님이 좋아하시는 것들을 갖다 드렸더니 아주 기뻐하셨다.
   Once a month I brought Father the things he likes, and he was very pleased.

7. 웃사람이 수저도 들기전에 밥상에 차린 음식이 삽시간에 없어 졌다.
   Before the seniors even lifted their spoons, the food on the table had disappeared in a flash.

Lesson Nine: Tensification and Voicing / 103

8. 학생이 꽃송이를 들고 나와 각 사람에게 나누어 주었다.
   The student came forward holding a bunch of flowers and gave one to each person.

9. 국수는 역시 그집 국수가 제일이다.
   If it's noodles you're talking about, that restaurant is the best.

10. 보내 준 잡지를 받고도 아직 답장을 하지 못했다.
    Even after receiving the magazine she had sent me, I wasn't able to write her back.

11. 복잡한 일이기 때문에 직접 만나서 의논하고 결정하려고 한다.
    Because it's a complicated business, I intend to meet him in person in order to discuss it and make a decision.

12. 늦지 않도록 이십분 전에 떠나자.
    Let's leave 20 minutes early so as not to be late.

13. 관광객들이 입국 수속을 마치고 안내자의 설명을 듣고 있다.
    Having completed the entrance formalities, the tourists are listening to their guide's explanations.

14. 일에 쫓기다가 독감에 걸리고 말았다.
    Harassed by work, I ended up catching the flu.

15. 개가 무슨 소리를 듣고 짖기 시작했다.
    Hearing some noise, the dog started barking.

16. 안방에 계신 할아버지 앞에서 담배를 피울 수 없어서 건넌방으로 건너 갔다.
    I couldn't smoke in front of grandfather in the *anpang* so I crossed over to the room opposite.

17. 방이 너무 추워서 방바닥에 깔아 놓은 이불 속에 들어가 영어 문법을 공부했다.
    The room was too cold, so I crawled under the bedding spread out on the floor and studied English grammar.

18. 침대에 누워서 12시가 넘도록 소설을 읽었다.
    I lay in bed reading a novel until past midnight.

19. 문득 군대 동기생들의 얼굴들이 떠 올랐다.
    Suddenly I recalled the faces of my Army buddies.

20. 그 아이는 용돈이 떨어져도 절대로 달라고 하지 않는다.
    Even when he runs out of pocket money, that child never asks for more.

21. 그녀는 꿈속에서 만났던 남성을 잊지 못하고 있다.
    She cannot forget the man she met in her dreams.

22. 손수 만든 손수건을 선물로 주었다.
    She gave away the handkerchief she had made herself.

23. 풍속을 몰라서 실수한 것을 항상 적어 둔다.
    I always keep a record of the mistakes I make due to my ignorance of the local customs.

24. 갑자기 급한 일이 생겨서 밤중에 김장을 하게 되었다.
    An urgent matter came up, so I ended up doing the *kimjang* in the middle of the night.

25. 중국 글자인 한자는 한글에 비해 어렵다고 할 수 있다.
    Compared to *han'gŭl*, it can be said that *hancca* which are Chinese characters, are more difficult.

26. 대가족제도의 장점과 단점을 말해 보자.
    Let's discuss the strengths and weaknesses of the large family system.

27. 실제로 아들자식보다 딸자식이 나을까?
    Do you suppose it's actually better to have girls than boys?

28. 금강산도 식후경이라지만, 잠깐 집 구경부터 하고 식사하자.
    They say "Even *Kŭmgangsan* should be seen on a full stomach", but let's have a quick tour of the house before we eat.

29. 연구 결과를 평한 것이지 그분의 인격을 무시한 것은 아니다.
    All I'm criticizing is her research results — I'm not running her down as a person.

30. 장가를 갔더니 아내가 아침마다 해장국을 끓여 준다.
    Now that I'm married, my wife makes *haejangkkuuk* for me every morning.

31. 길가에 앉아 물건을 파는 사람들의 수입은 하루에 얼마나 될까?
    How do you suppose the daily income is of the people who sit out on the street and sell their goods?

Lesson Ten

Aspiration

Before or after ㅎ, the Plain consonants ㅂ, ㄷ, ㅈ and ㄱ become aspirates and are pronounced ㅍ, ㅌ, ㅊ, ㅋ respectively.

Chart 12. **Aspiration**

ㅂ				ㅍ				
ㄷ	+	ㅎ	→	ㅌ	←	ㅎ	+	ㄷ
ㅈ				ㅊ				ㅈ
ㄱ				ㅋ				ㄱ

1. /p + h/ → [pʰ]

입학	[이팍]
협회	[혀푀]
급행	[그팽]
합하다	[하파다]
급히	[그피]
좁히다	[조피다]
넓히다	[널피다]

Lesson Ten: Aspiration / 107

2. /t + h, h + t/→ [tʰ]

맏형	[마텽]	낳더군	[나터군]
몇해	[며태]	좋디	[조티]
윷한다	[유탄다]	빨갛다	[빨가타]
꽃향기	[꼬턍기]	놓도록	[노토록]
못한다	[모탄다]	자그맣다	[자그마타]
옷 한벌	[오탄벌]	않던	[안턴]
낮 한때	[나탄때]	싫다	[실타]
꽃 한 송이	[꼬탄송이]	많더군	[만터군]

3. /ts + h, h + ts/→ [tsʰ]

앉히다	[안치다]	그렇지	[그러치]	놓지	[노치]
맞히다	[마치다]	좋지요	[조치요]	쌓지요	[싸치요]
엎혀살다	[언쳐살다]	빨갛지	[빨가치]	닿지	[달치]
잊혀지다	[이쳐지다]	노랗지	[노라치]
꽃혔다	[꼬쳗따]	싫지	[실치]

4. /k + h, h + k/→ [kʰ]

각하	[가카]	좋고	[조코]
북한	[부칸]	놓게	[노케]
먹히다	[머키다]	많군	[만쿤]
축하하다	[추카하다]	싫고	[실코]

생각하다 [생가카다]   귀찮게 [귀찬케]
똑똑하다 [똑또카다]   점잖게 [점잔케]
먹히다 [머키다]   파랗구나 [파라쿠나]
역할 [여칼]

Lesson Ten: Aspiration / 109

Exercise 20. Read the following sentences out loud, paying careful attention to Aspiration.

1. **입학한** 지 엊그제 같은데 벌써 졸**업하**다니?
   It seems like only yesterday since he entered university; you mean to say he's graduated already?

2. 김치독이 땅에 **묻혀** 있습니다.
   The *Kimchi* jars are buried beneath the ground.

3. **급한** 일이 생겨서 **급행**열차를 타고 갔다.
   An emergnecy came up, so I went on an express train.

4. 이 나무는 **몇 해**만에 꽃이 피었습니까?
   How many years has it been since this tree last gave flowers?

5. 빨**갛고 꽃향**기가 좋은 꽃으로 사오세요.
   Buy some nice bright red flowers that smell good.

6. **착한** 사람은 복을 받는다.
   Good people are blessed.

7. 선생 나라의 **국화**는 무엇입니까?
   What is the national flower of your country?

8. 그는 어릴 적부터 똑**똑하**고 재주가 있었다.
   From a young age, he was bright and talented.

9. **좋지** 않은 일은 빨리 잊어야 하는데 **잊혀**지지 않는다.
   One should forget unpleasant things, but they just won't go away.

10. 활을 잘 쏜다고 들었는데 무엇이든지 잘 **맞힐** 수 있어요?
    I've heard you're good with a bow [and arrow]; can you hit anything pretty well?

11. 그는 일등으로 **뽑혀서** 상을 받았다.
    He was selected as Number One and received a prize.

12. 그의 생각이 **좋지 않다**고 허락하지 않는다.
    They won't give him permission because they think his idea is

III. Phonological Changes

Exercise 21. Fill in the blanks with the Korean word as actually pronounced.

1. 오늘은 입학식이 있어서 일찍 출근했다.
           (   )
   Today is the Entrance Ceremony, so I left early for work.

2. 너무 급하게 서둘러서 결과가 좋지 않았다.
         (   )   (   )
   I rushed about too hastily, so the result was no good.

3. 몇 해 동안 맏형을 만나지 못했다.
   (   ) (   )   (   )
   I haven't seen my eldest brother for several years.

4. 좋고 좋던 시절이 다 지나갔다.
   (   )(   )
   The good old days have gone.

5. 작년에 입학했다가 1년 휴학했다.
         (   )
   I entered university last year but then took a year off.

6. 어떻게 축하해 줄까 하고 생각중이다.
   (   )(   )
   I'm in the middle of considering how to congratulate you.

7. 귀찮게 굴던 그 사람이 잊혀지지 않는다.
   (   )   (   )
   I can't forget that person who behaved so annoyingly.

8. 꽃향기가 너무나 좋구나.
   (   )   (   )
   The flowers smell so nice!

9. 단풍이 들어서 산이 빨갛고 노랗지?
   (   ) (   )

   The mountains are red and yellow with the autumn colors, aren't they?

10. 그 물건이 생각했던 것보다 좋지 못했어.
    (   )   (   )

    Those goods weren't as good as I had imagined.

Lesson Eleven

Palatalization

When a syllable-final ㄷ or ㅌ meets a following /i/ or /j/, it is pronounced as ㅈ or ㅊ, respectively. This is called Palatalization.

1. /t + i/ → [tsi]

맏 + 이 → 맏이   [마지]
굳 + 이 → 굳이   [구지]
곧 + 이 → 곧이   [고지]
해돋 + 이 → 해돋이 [해도지]
땀받 + 이 → 땀받이 [땀바지]
미닫 + 이 → 미닫이 [미다지]
여닫 + 이 → 여닫이 [여다지]

2. /tʰ + i/ → [tsʰi]

같 + 이 → 같이   [가치]
밑 + 이 → 밑이   [미치]
끝 + 이 → 끝이   [끄치]
밭 + 이 → 밭이   [바치]
햇볕 + 이 → 햇볕이 [핸뼈치, 해뼈치]
바깥 + 이 → 바깥이 [바까치]
핥 + 이다 → 핥이다 [할치다]

낱낱 + 이 → 낱낱이 [난나치]

3. /t + h + i/ → [tsʰi]

In this case, ㄷ + ㅎ first undergo Aspiration, and then the resulting ㅌ goes on to undergo Palatalization.

묻 + 히다 → 묻히다 [무치다]
묻 + 히어서 → 묻혀서 [무쳐서]
걷 + 히다 → 걷히다 [거치다]
닫 + 히어서 → 닫혀서 [다쳐서]
닫 + 히다 → 닫히다 [다치다]
갇 + 히어서 → 갇혀서 [가쳐서]
받 + 히다 → 받히다 [바치다]
갇 + 히다 → 갇히다 [가치다]
굳 + 히다 → 굳히다 [구치다]

114 / III. Phonological Changes

Exercise 22. Read the following sentences out loud, paying careful attention to Palatalization.

1. 우리는 밭으로 들어가 농부들을 도왔는데, **밭이** 크지 않아 일은 쉽게 끝났다.
   We went into the field and helped the farmers, but the field was not very big, so the work was easily finished.

2. 오늘 안으로 일을 끝내려고 부지런히 했는데도 **끝이** 나지 않아 중도에서 그쳤다.
   Although we worked hard so as to finish the work by the end of today, we didn't finish, and knocked off in the middle.

3. 가을이라 바람은 선선하지만 **햇볕이** 뜨거워서 바깥에 나가기가 싫다.
   There is a cool breeze because it's autumn, but the sun is hot, so I don't want to go outside.

4. 맏아들이 어깨가 무겁다고 하는 것은 **맏이**가 해야 할 일이 많아서 일까?
   Does your eldest son say his shoulders feel heavy because there are so many things an eldest son should do?

5. 엄마 개구리는 산에 **묻히**고 싶어서 엄마 말에 반대로만 하는 개구리 형제에게 자기를 물가에 묻으라고 하고는 눈을 감았다.
   Because the mother frog wanted to be buried in the mountains, before dying she told the frog brothers, who always did the opposite of what she said, to bury her beside the river.

6. 굳은 약속을 했다고 열이 많은데도 **굳이** 고집을 부리고 약속 장소로 나갔다.
   In spite of his high fever, he stubbornly appeared at the meeting place because he had made a firm commitment.

Lesson Eleven: Palatalization / 115

7. 하도 거짓말을 잘 하니까 그 사람 말을 **곧이**듣는 사람이 없다.
   Because he is such a great liar, nobody takes him at his word.

8. 석굴암에 갔다가 **해돋이**도 못 보고 오다니! 기회가 있으면 해 돋는 것 꼭 가서 보고 오세요.
   You went to *Sŏkkuram* and didn't even see the sunrise! If you get the chance, you absolutely must go and see the sunrise.

9. 끝 없이 걸어 갔는데도 **끝이** 없잖겠어요? 그래서 택시를 타자고 했어요.
   Even though we had walked endlessly, there comes no end in sight, so I suggested we take a taxi.

10. **바같이** 추울텐데 바같에서 뭘 하고 있어요?
    What are they doing outside.....It must be cold.

11. 문이 **닫혀** 있는데, 창문으로 들어가게 저 좀 **받혀** 주시겠어요?
    The door is locked; will you lift me up so I can go in through the window?

Exercise 23. Read the following sentences out loud, and fill in the blanks with the Korean word as actually pronounced.

1. 그는 내 말을 언제나 곧이듣지 않는다.
   (   )
   He never takes me seriously.

2. 그는 나의 도움을 굳이 사양한다.
   (   )
   He steadfastly declines my help.

3. 요즘 해돋이 시간이 몇 시지?
   (   )
   What time is the sunrise these days?

4. 이 옷은 땀받이로 샀는데 썩 좋지 않다.
   (   )
   I bought this to use as an undershirt, but it's really no good.

5. 그는 누구의 말이라도 곧이곧대로 믿는다.
   (   )
   He takes absolutely everybody at their word.

6. 형제중에 맏이의 키가 제일 작다.
   (   )
   Among our brothers the eldest is the shortest.

7. 바닷가로 나가서 해돋이 구경하자.
   (   )
   Let's go to the seashore and watch the sunrise.

8. 내가 굳이 그 집까지 갈 필요가 있을까?
   (   )
   Is it really absolutely necessary for me to go to that house?

9. 집안에서 뒷곁이 훤히 내다보인다.
             (   )

   The whole back yard is visible from inside the house.

10. 밭이 넓어서 여럿이 같이 씨를 뿌렸다.
    (   )   (   )

    It was a large field, so several people sowed the seeds together.

11. 조상이 묻힌 묘를 찾을 수 없었다.
          (   )

    I was unable to find the grave where my ancestors are buried.

12. 미닫이 문을 열고 내다보니까 나무에 싹이 돋아나고 있었다.
    (   )

    When I slid open the sliding door and looked out, there were buds sprouting on the tree.

13. 안개가 걷히기 시작했다.
          (   )

    The fog has started to lift.

14. 도둑이 닫힌 문을 부수고 들어왔다.
          (   )

    The thief smashed the locked door and came in.

15. 이 이야기는 끝이 없다.
              (   )

    This story is endless.

IV.
Intrusive ㅅ and ㄴ

    Sometimes when two morphemes or words combine to form a compound, certain pronunciation changes occur at the boundary between the two elements. Most often, this pronunciation change involves tensification of an initial plain ㅂ, ㄷ, ㅈ, ㅅ, ㄱ in the second element of the compound. Korean spelling indicates this tensification only part of the time, namely, in cases where the first morpheme/word ends in a vowel. Korean spelling indicates the change in pronunciation by writing ㅅ at the end of the first element, and calls this ㅅ 'Intrusive ㅅ' (사이시옷).

Lesson Twelve

Insertion of ㅅ and ㄴ

1. ㅅ Insertion

When the first word/morpheme of a compound ends in a vowel, Korean writing often adds an ㅅ at the end of the first element (there are also many exceptions; basically, you have to learn this on a word-by-word basis).

1) If the second morpheme/word begins with this ㅂ, ㄷ, ㅈ, ㅅ, ㄱ, this is tensified (see p. 99).

내	+	가	→	냇가	→	낻가	[낻까, 내까]
새	+	길	→	샛길	→	샏길	[샏낄, 새낄]
빨래	+	돌	→	빨랫돌	→	빨랟돌	[빨랟똘, 빨래똘]
코	+	등	→	콧등	→	곧등	[곧뜽, 코뜽]
기	+	발	→	깃발	→	긷발	[긷빨, 기빨]
대패	+	밥	→	대팻밥	→	대팯밥	[대팯빱, 대패빱]
초	+	불	→	촛불	→	촏불	[촏뿔, 초뿔]
해	+	빛	→	햇빛	→	핻빛	[핻삗, 해삗]
배	+	사공	→	뱃사공	→	밷사공	[밷싸공, 배싸공]
해	+	살	→	햇살	→	핻살	[핻쌀, 해쌀]
배	+	속	→	뱃속	→	밷속	[밷쏙, 배쏙]
배	+	전	→	뱃전	→	밷전	[밷쩐, 배쩐]
고개	+	짓	→	고갯짓	→	고갣진	[고갣찓, 고개찓]

2) If the second morpheme/word begins with ㅁ or ㄴ, the ㅅ assimilates first to ㄷ, then on to ㄴ (see P. 90).

이 + 몸 → 잇몸 → 인몸 [인몸, 임몸]
비 + 물 → 빗물 → 빈물 [빈물, 빔물]
배 + 머리 → 뱃 머리 → 밴 머리 [밴 머리, 뱀 머리]
뒤 + 모양 → 뒷 모양 → 뒨 모양 [뒨 모양, 뒴 모양]
아래 + 목 → 아랫 목 → 아랜 목 [아랜 목, 아램 목]
퇴 + 마루 → 툇마루 → 퇸마루 [퇸마루, 툄마루]

코 + 날 → 콧날 → 콘날 [콘날]
배 + 놈 → 뱃놈 → 밴놈 [밴놈]
코 + 노래 → 콧 노래 → 콘 노래 [콘 노래]
배 + 놀이 → 뱃 놀이 → 밴 놀이 [밴 노리]
아래 + 냇가 → 아랫 냇가 → 아랜 낻가 → [아랜 낻까, 아랜 내까]

2. ㄴ Insertion

When the first morpheme/word ends in a consonant, and the following element begins with / i / or / y / (이, 야, 여, 요, 유), Korean pronunciation inserts an ㄴ to the following elements: 니, 냐, 녀, 뇨, 뉴.

a) When the second element begins with 이

ㄱ– *patčhim*

In this case, the final ㄱ assimilates to ㅇ before the intrusive ㄴ.

속 + 잎 → 속 닢 [송닙]
막 + 일 → 막 닐 [망닐]

부엌 + 일 → 부억 닐 [부엉 닐]
흙 + 일 → 흙닐 → 흑 닐 [홍 닐]
샀 + 일 → 샀 닐 → 삭 닐 [상 닐]

ㄴ – *patčhim*

어떤 + 일 [어떤 닐]
논 + 일 [논 닐]
잔 + 일 [잔 닐]
맨 + 입 [맨 닙]
한 + 일 [한 닐]

ㄷ – *patčhim*

In this case, the final ㄷ assimilates to ㄴ before the intrusive ㄴ.

못 + 잊어 → 몯 닞어 [몬 니저]
낮 + 일 → 낟 닐 [난 닐]
꽃 + 이름 → 꼳 니름 [꼰 니름]
꽃 + 잎 → 꼳 닢 [꼰 닙]
밭 + 이랑 → 받 니랑 [반 니랑]
낯 + 익은 → 낟 닉은 [난 니근]
홑 + 이불 → 혿 니불 [혼 니불]
옷 + 입다 → 옫 닙다 [온 닙따]

ㄹ – *patčhim*

In this case, the intrusive ㄴ after the final ㄹ assimilates to ㄹ, giving a double ㄹㄹ.

솔 + 잎 → 솔닙 [솔립]
열 + 일곱 → 열 닐곱 [열 릴곱]
할 + 일 → 할 닐 [할 릴]
들 + 일 → 들 닐 [들 릴]

설 + 익다 → 설 닉다　[설 릭따]
잘 + 입다 → 잘 닙다　[잘 립따, 자 립따]

ㅁ– *patčhim*

금　+ 이　　[금 니]
밤　+ 일　　[밤 닐]
밤　+ 이슬　[밤 니슬]
솜　+ 이불　[솜 니불]
여름 + 이불　[여름 니불]

ㅂ– *patčhim*

In this case, the final ㅂ assimilates to ㅁ before the intrusive ㄴ.

집 + 일 → 집 닐　[짐 닐]
앞 + 일 → 압 닐　[암 닐]
앞 + 이 → 압 니　[암 니]

ㅇ– *patčhim*

가랑 + 잎　[가랑 닙]
사랑 + 이　[사랑 니]
콩　+ 잎　[콩 닙]

b) When the second element begins with 야, 여, 요, 유.

내복 + 약　→ 내복 냑　[내봉 냑]
무슨 + 약　→ 무슨 냑　[무슨 냑]

저녁 + 연기 → 저녁 년기　[저녕 년기]
색　+ 연필 → 색 년필　　[생 년필]
부산 + 역　→ 부산녁　　[부산녁]
한　+ 여름 → 한 녀름　　[한 녀름]

신   + 여성 → 신 녀성   [신 녀성]
설흔 + 여섯 → 설흔 녀섯   [서른 녀선]
먹은 + 엿 → 먹은 녓   [머근 녇]
남존 + 여비 → 남존녀비   [남존녀비]
첫   + 여름 → 첫 녀름 → 쳔 녀름 [천 녀름]
늦   + 여름 → 늦 녀름 → 는 녀름 [는 녀름]
꿀   + 엿 → 꿀 녓 → 꿀 녇 [꿀렫]
불   + 여우 → 불녀우   [불려우]
물   + 엿 → 물 녓 → 물 녇 [물렫]
서울 + 역 → 서울녁   [서울력]
스물 + 여섯 → 스물녀섯 → 스물녀섣 [스물려섣]
먹을 + 엿 → 먹을 녓 → 먹을 녇 [머글 렫]
암   + 여우 → 암 녀우   [암 녀우]
숲   + 옆 → 숲 녚 → 숩 녑 [숨 녑]
장   + 옆 → 장 녚 → 장 녑 [장 녑]
콩   + 엿 → 콩 녓 → 콩 녇 [콩 녇]
직행 + 열차 → 직행녈차   [지캥 녈차]

무슨 + 요일 → 무슨 뇨일   [무슨 뇨일]
눈   + 요기 → 눈 뇨기   [눈 뇨기]
담   + 요 → 담뇨   [담뇨]
영업 + 용 → 영업 뇽   [영엄 뇽]

식용 + 유 → 식용뉴   [시콩뉴]
휘발 + 유 → 휘발뉴   [휘발류]
국민 + 윤리 → 국민뉼리   [궁민뉼리]

IV. Intrusive ㅅ and ㄴ

Exercise 24. Read the following sentences out loud, paying careful attention to intrusive ㅅ and ㄴ.

1. 바**닷가**에 앉아 **햇빛**을 쬐고 싶다.
   I want to sit at the seaside and bask in the sun.

2. 나**뭇잎**이 바람에 떨어져 **냇가**에 가득히 쌓였다.
   The tree leaves have fallen in the wind and are piled up high at the edge of the stream.

3. **뱃머**리에 앉아 노를 젖고 있는 여학생의 **뒷모습**이 영숙이 같다.
   From behind, the female student sitting at the bow of the boat and rowing looks like Yŏngsuk.

4. 갑자기 소나기가 쏟아져 머리에서 **빗물**이 뚝뚝 떨어진다.
   There was a sudden shower, and rain water is dripping from my hair.

5. **앞일**을 생각하여 자리에서 곧 일어났다.
   Thinking of things to come, I got up immediately from my seat.

6. 병원에서 **낮 일**을 하는 줄 알고 찾아 갔더니 **밤 일**을 한다고 해서 못 만나고 돌아왔다.
   Thinking she was working days at the hospital, I went to see her, but they said she was working nights, so I came back without meeting her.

7. 부엌 **일**보다 바깥 **일**이 쉽지 않을까?
   Don't you think outdoor work is easier than kitchen work?

8. **논 일**을 끝내 놓고 **잔 일**을 이것 저것 하고 나니까 밤 10시가 되었다.
   After finishing the work in the rice paddy and then doing odd

jobs of this and that, it was already ten at night.

9. **사랑이**가 나느라고 **잇몸**이 잔뜩 부었다.
   My gums are all swollen because of my wisdom teeth coming in.

10. 무**슨 약**인지 **물약**만 가지고 왔다.
    I don't know what kind of medicine it is, but all she brought was a liquid medicine.

11. 일**산역**에 내리니까 집집마다 굴뚝에서 저**녁 연**기가 나오고 있었다.
    When I got off at Ilsan Station, evening smoke was coming out of the chimneys of all the houses.

12. **늦여**름 장마는 농사에 이롭지 못하다.
    The late summer rainy season is not good for farming.

13. **콩엿**을 만들었는데 어쩌면 이렇게 **꿀엿**이에요?
    We made bean taffy — how come this is honey taffy?

V.
Prosodic Features

Lesson Thirteen

Length, Pitch and Stress

1. Length

In standard Korean, vowels can be either short or long, and the meaning of words is sometimes distinguished according to whether the vowel is long or short. Vowel length is distinctive this way in Korean chiefly in first syllables (though even here, it is dying out among younger speakers).

Long Vowel		Short Vowel	
밤 나무	chestnut tree	밤 길	street at night
말씨	way of speaking	말 타기	horse-riding
눈 사람	snowman	눈물	tears
감사하다	to thank	감사원	inspector
과장하다	to exaggerate	과장님	Department Chief
김밥	*kimpap*	김씨	surname Kim
시장	market	시장하다	be hungry
거리가 멀다	distance is far	거리에 나와 놀다	come out and play in street
차관을 얻었다	got a loan	문교부 차관이다	is Vice-Minister in the Ministry of Education
힘이 센 장수이다	is a strong generalissimo	과일 장수이다	is a fruit peddler

2. Pitch

Modern Seoul Korean has lost the distinctive Highs and Lows in pitch which made up the pitch-accent system of 15th-century Korean, but pitch contours are important at the sentence level for their role in intonation. Thus, pitch intonations at the end of a sentence often signal whether the sentence is a statement, question, command and so on. Yes-no questions finish high, but questions asking for information typically go down in pitch at the end. In connected speech, Korean intonation tends to be rather flat and monotonous, especially in official or public modes (TV and radio announcements, etc).

We can divide Korean intonation pitches into three types: Rising, Falling and Level.

    Rising pitch indicates: a yes-no question
    Falling pitch indicates: a statement, order, invitation
                                    or information question
    Level pitch indicates: that the speaker isn't finished yet

편지를 쓰십니까?   ↑
Are you writing a letter?

어디에 가십니까?   ↑, ↓
Where are you going?

공항에 나갑니다.   ↓
I'm going out to the airport.

먼저 드십시오.   ↓
Go ahead and eat first.

같이 갑시다.   ↓
Let's go together.

지금 바쁜데... →
I'm rather busy now...

In an alternative question, the first question ends on a Rising pitch, and the second on a Falling pitch.

이것이 술입니까, ↑   물입니까? ↓
Is this booze, or water?

음악회에 갈까요, ↑   연극을 볼까요? ↓
Shall we go to a concert, or a play?

3. Stress

Stress is essentially the amplitude of the sounds produced by the vibrations of the vocal chords. When we speak, we use stress to give special prominence to certain sounds, thus playing up some, and playing down others. This lends a kind of rhythm to speech and makes it more pleasant to listen to; without rises and falls in amplitude, it would be monotonous and more difficult to understand.

1) Rhythm in standard Korean comes from the interplay of long and short sounds. Typically, in a 2, 3 or 4-syllable sequence, the rhythm goes "Strong-Weak-Weak" or "Weak-Strong-Weak".

Strong Weak Weak
<u>쇠</u>고기
<u>사</u>람들
<u>교</u>육
<u>전</u>화
<u>감</u>사합니다
<u>죄</u>송합니다

Weak Strong Weak
화장실
자전거
문학
기차
전합니다
방학입니다

2) Stress in Korean is different from accent in English, and attaches to certain words in a Korean *sentence* (English accent operates on syllables at the *word* level). Korean stress does not distinguish words from one another, but rather expresses either the speaker's attitude toward what he is saying, his emotions, or else simply emphasis.

'우리는 '밥을 먹고 '삽니다.
'우리는 밥을 '먹고 삽니다.
'저기 가서 그 '앨 데리고 오십시오.
'저기 가서 그 앨 '데리고 오십시오.

Lesson Thirteen: Length, Pitch and Stress / *135*

Exercise 25. Read the following sentences out loud.(- for short, = for long)

1. 어제 밤에 늦게까지 책을 읽었다.
   I read a book until late.

   대보름에는 호도 잣 땅콩 밤등을 먹는다.
   On Tae Borŭm (Jan. 15th by the lunar calendar), we eat walnuts, pine nuts, peanuts, chestnuts, etc.

2. 발이 아파서 혼났다.
   My feet hurt incredibly.

   문은 열어 놓고 발을 쳐.
   Open the door and let down the bamboo blind.

3. 김치에 굴을 넣어야 맛이 있다.
   You have to put oysters in *Kimchi* for it to taste good.

   신촌으로 가려면 굴을 지나야 간다.
   If you want to go to Shinch'on, you have to pass through a tunnel.

4. 눈이 아프면 병원에 가.
   If your eye hurts, go to the hospital!

   밖에 눈이 온다.
   It's snowing outside.

5. 죄를 지었으면 벌을 받아야지.
   If you've committted a sin, you must be punished.

   벌이 손등을 쏘았어.
   A bee stung me on the hand.

6. 거리에 나와서 장사를 하고 있다.
   He's come out into the street and is doing business.

거기는 거리가 멀어서 걸어 갈 수 없다.
That place is far away, so we can't go by foot.

7. 여자는 가정을 지켜야지.
   Women should be home-makers.

   이 문제는 해결할 수 있다고 가정하자.
   Let's suppose this problem can be resolved.

8. 밥을 국에다 말아 먹었다.
   I put my rice in the soup and ate it.

   길에서 놀지 말고 집에서 놀아라.
   Play in the house, not in the street.

9. 애기를 업어 주어라.
   Carry the baby on your back.

   애기가 없어서 걱정이야.
   I'm worried that they have no children.

10. 비가 오니 빨래를 걷어요.
    It's raining—bring in the laundry!

    빨리 걷지 늦겠다.
    Walk quickly — we'll be late!

11. 일하는 김씨는 김밥을 가지고 다닙니다.
    The Kim who works here carries *kimpap* with him.

Index

affricates	22
alveolar	27
alveo-palatal	22
aspirated consonants	23
aspiration	106
back vowels	16
bilabials	22
central vowels	16
complex *patchim*	51
consonant assimilations	86
consonants	22
contraction	79
diphthongs	19
distinctions of consonants	22
falling pitch	132
following vowel	79
fricatives	22
front vowels	16
glottal	28
high vowels	16
length	131
level pitch	132
liquid sound	22
long vowel	131
loss	79, 81
low vowels	16
mid vowels	16
nasal sounds	22
obligatory	79

optional	79
palatalization	112
patchim	39
phonemes of Korean	13
phonological changes	73
pitch	132
places of articulation	27
plain sounds	22
plosives	22
preceding vowel	79
prosodic features	129
rising pitch	132
rounded vowels	15
short vowel	131
simple vowels	15
stress	133
syllable	39
tense consonants	23
tensification	96
tongue height	16
tongue position	16
tongue-tip	22
ŭmsŏng vowels	76
unrounded vowels	15
voicing	96
voiced consonants	68
voiced sounds	22
voiceless consonants	68
voiceless sounds	22
vowel harmony	75
vowels	15
yangsŏng vowels	76
ㄴ insertion	122
ㅅ insertion	121

한국어 발음

2001년 9월 15일 1판 2쇄

저 자 : 연세대학교 한국어학당 편
발 행 : 연 세 대 학 교　출 판 부
서울특별시 서대문구 신촌동 134
전 화　392-6201
　　　　2123-3380～2
FAX　393-1421
e-mail : ysup@yonsei.ac.kr
등 록　1955년 10월 13일 제9-60호
인 쇄　태화인쇄주식회사

ISBN 89-7141-395-6　　　값 4,500원